EXCLUSIVITY REBATES AS ABUSE OF DOMINANT POSITION

Analysis of the EU General Court's judgment in *Intel*

EXCLUSIVITY REBATES AS ABUSE OF DOMINANT POSITION

Analysis of the EU General Court's judgment in *Intel*

Ricardo Botelho

EDITORA SINGULAR

2016

Dados Internacionais de Catalogação na Publicação (CIP)

B748e

Botelho, Ricardo

Exclusivity rebates as abuse of dominant position: analysis of the EU General Court's judgment in *Intel*. / Ricardo Botelho. São Paulo: Singular, 2016.

186 p.

ISBN: 978-85-86626-87-6

1. Direito da Concorrência. 2. Abuso do Poder Econômico. 3. Descontos Condicionados. 4. Exclusividade. 5. Direito Europeu. 6. Direito Econômico. I. Título.

CDU: 339.923

Texto revisto pelo Autor
Diagramação e Capa: Microart Design Editorial

Cover Image: Turner, J.M.W. 1839. *The Fighting Temeraire tugged to her last berth to be broken up*. Oil on canvas. The National Gallery, London

Editora Singular
Rua Cardoso de Almeida, 788, cj 121
05013-001 – São Paulo-SP
Tel. (11) 3872-2609
www.editorasingular.com.br
singular@editorasingular.com.br

All that is meant cannot be expressed
in a dedication.

This book is dedicated to Juliana and Catarina,
for everything.

Summary

Few topics in competition law are as controversial as rebate practices by dominant undertakings. And few cases in EU case-law have originated as much vivid debates as the General Court's judgment of June 2014 in *Intel*.

Careful examination of the legal standards established in the judgment – which is the object of this book – is crucial for mapping parameters to guide undertakings concerned about application of competition law on abuse of dominance to rebate practices, particularly to exclusivity rebates – that is, rebates conditional to customers obtaining all or most of their requirements from the dominant undertaking.

The analysis reveals that the central element of the legal assessment in the judgment is the affirmation of the anticompetitive nature of exclusivity rebates by dominant undertakings. The rejection of the 'as-efficient competitor' analysis as part of the legal test of exclusivity rebates – a novel issue in EU jurisprudence and which has originated so much debate – is only a logical consequence of this understanding.

Although not a surprise (because in harmony with settled EU case-law), the General Court's judgment in *Intel* is a setback for those expecting a radical shift towards the 'effects-based' standards used in the European Commission's *Guidance on Enforcement Priorities.* The judgment does not imply, however, that the *Guidance*'s standards are useless when it comes to assessing exclusivity rebates. On the contrary, they will continue to be applicable to exclusivity rebates according to their original purposes: priority settings.

The Court's reasons for declaring the inapplicability of any *de minimis* threshold under the European law of abuse of dominance (Article 102 TFEU) and for finding exclusivity even when only a specific segment of the market is affected, however, are unconvincing and raise practical concerns. Except for these topics, it seems a sensible decision on legal and economic grounds, as it properly identifies exclusivity – and not low price – as the source of harm to competition resulting from exclusivity rebates by dominant undertakings.

Preface

I was delighted to be asked to write a Preface to Ricardo Botelho's excellent book on Exclusivity Rebates as Abuse of Dominant Position; the book originated in an MA dissertation conducted under my supervision at King's College London in academic year 2014/2015. As the author says in the Introduction of his book, few topics in competition law are as controversial as this one. Competition law today has many challenges – adaptation of the existing law on vertical agreements to the burgeoning world of e-commerce; the extent to which the competition rules should be applied to rapidly evolving high technology markets; how to determine what is a FRAND-royalty for the licensing of standard-essential patents. A vast amount of thinking has gone into these, and many other, new and challenging questions. And yet one of the most difficult and contentious subjects remains the appropriate standard for the assessment of rebates when offered by firms with 'substantial market power' or, as many legal systems are written, dominant firms. In the EU two judgments of the Court of Justice in the 1970s – the *Sugar Cartel* case and *Hoffmann-la Roche v Commission* – established that exclusive purchasing agreements entered into by a dominant firm could infringe Article 102 TFEU (or, at that time, Article 86 of the EEC Treaty). The reasoning was that exclusivity could foreclose access to the market for the dominant firm's competitors; for this reason it was irrelevant that the customer might be perfectly willing to be subject to the exclusivity condition: the purpose of the law was to ensure access to the market, not to protect the customer as such. It followed naturally that the Court in these judgments also took exception to rebates conditional upon exclusivity: otherwise the simple device of dropping a contractual term demanding exclusivity but replacing it with a clear economic incentive to purchase exclusively would make evasion of the law too easy.

But is the treatment of exclusivity rebates as simple as that? A rebate is a price cut, and competition law for the most part encourages competition that leads to lower prices. Predatory pricing – charging prices below cost – can amount to abusive behaviour, but the law on predation demands a careful consideration of 'domco's' prices and costs: normally only pricing below an appropriate measure of cost – average variable cost/average avoidable cost/long-run average incremental cost – will be found to be unlawful. Many commentators argue that it should follow that only rebates that involve some element of below-cost behaviour should be found to be unlawful: in other words, the law on rebates should be 'detached' from the ban on exclusivity and 'attached' to the law of predation. Proponents of this view are fortified in their criticism of the law by criticizing the 'formalism' of the case-law emanating from the *Sugar Cartel* and *Hoffmann-la Roche* and arguing instead for a more 'effects'-based system, and one which protects only firms as-efficient or more efficient than domco, and not less efficient ones.

This is the essence of the debate, and it is one that has raged for a long time, in the EU, the US and beyond; and also *between* the EU and the US. The European Commission's *Guidance on Enforcement Priorities under Article 102 TFEU* seemed to indicate a clear intention on its part to move towards a more effects-based treatment of rebates by dominant firms, based on the as-efficient competitor principle. However it is ultimately for the Court of Justice, not the Commission, to determine the actual content of the law. We now find ourselves at a crucial moment for this debate: the Commission's decision in *Intel* – a case that was initiated before the *Guidance* paper – concluded that Intel was guilty of using exclusivity rebates (and of other abusive practices); that decision was upheld by the General Court in 2014: as the author says, this was a setback for those expecting a radical shift in the law. The *Intel* judgment is the main focus of this book. The case is now on appeal before the Court of Justice, and its judgment is eagerly awaited. My expectation is that the Court of Justice will uphold the General Court's judgment on the issue of rebates; however I am less certain what will be the outcome of a separate point that is on appeal, namely the jurisdictional reach of EU law in a case where a US firm offers rebates to a Chinese OEM that incorporates Intel's chips into its own products in China. Meanwhile, in 2015 the Court of Justice handed down a judgment on rebates under Article 102 TFEU in a case that was referred to it by a Danish Court, *Post Danmark (II)*, and it seems to me that this judgment says nothing new on the topic of rebates to offer hope to Intel in its appeal. Fascinatingly the Commission has recently sent a statement of objections to Qualcomm of the US, accusing it of granting abusive exclusivity rebates; this case will be watched with close interest in the light of the *Intel* and *Post Danmark (II)* judgments.

Ricardo Botelho's book explores these fascinating issues, and it is being published at an excellent time, given the subject's topicality. I am sure that practising lawyers and economists in Brazil as well as judges, officials and academics will find it to be of great value. I look forward to seeing how the treatment of dominant firms' rebating practices will evolve in Brazil and the rest of Latin America in the years ahead.

Richard Whish, QC (Hon)
Emeritus Professor of Law
King's College London

Contents

1
Introduction

The application of Article 102 of the Treaty on the Functioning of the European Union (TFEU)[1] to conditional rebates has long been one of the most controversial topics in EU competition law. While the case-law in the EU Courts has evolved based on an essentially formal approach, rejecting the need for case-specific qualitative or quantitative demonstration of anticompetitive effects to determine the existence of a violation of Article 102 TFEU, it has also been criticised for alleged poor alignment with sound (or modern) economic thinking[2].

The European Commission's *Guidance on the Commission's enforcement priorities in applying Article [102 TFEU] to abusive exclusionary conduct by dominant undertakings* ('the *Guidance on Enforcement Priorities*' or 'the *Guidance*')[3] clearly pointed in the direction of a so-called 'effects-

1. European Union competition law system is based on four legal pillars: the prohibition of cartels (Article 101 TFEU), the prohibition of abuse of a dominant position (Article 102 TFEU), the prohibition of anticompetitive concentrations between undertakings (Article 2(3) Regulation 139/2004), and the prohibition of state aid (Article 107 TFEU). Article 102 TFEU (ex Article 82 TEC) provides as follows: "Any abuse by one or more undertakings of a dominant position within the internal market or in a substantial part of it shall be prohibited as incompatible with the internal market in so far as it may affect trade between Member States. Such abuse may, in particular, consist in: (a) directly or indirectly imposing unfair purchase or selling prices or other unfair trading conditions; (b) limiting production, markets or technical development to the prejudice of consumers; (c) applying dissimilar conditions to equivalent transactions with other trading parties, thereby placing them at a competitive disadvantage; (d) making the conclusion of contracts subject to acceptance by the other parties of supplementary obligations which, by their nature or according to commercial usage, have no connection with the subject of such contracts".
2. See detailed discussion in section 3.2 below.
3. OJ [2009] C 45/7.

based' approach to exclusionary conducts, including conditional rebates, at least for the purposes of priority settings. Although it does not (and could not) state the law[4], the *Guidance* has created some expectation that its prioritisation tests would serve as inspiration for the EU Courts to change the case-law on conditional rebates under Article 102 towards an approach based on a more detailed analysis of anticompetitive effects.

This context makes the *Intel* case central to the discussion of the legal standards applicable to the assessment of conditional rebates under Article 102, in particular to exclusivity rebates – that is, rebates conditional to customers obtaining all or most of their requirements from the dominant undertaking.

In the judgment of 12 June 2014 ('the *Intel* judgment')[5], the General Court of the European Union upheld in its entirety the Commission's decision of 13 May 2009 ('the Commission's decision')[6], which imposed a fine of €1.06 billion on Intel for having abused its dominant position in the market for x86 central processing units (CPUs). In summary, the General Court upheld the Commission's findings that Intel had granted rebates to four major global computer manufacturers (Dell, HP, NEC and Lenovo) and had made payments to the retailer Media Saturn Holding (MSH)[7] conditional to their exclusivity or quasi-exclusivity, and had made payments to HP, Acer and Lenovo for their abandoning or delaying the launch, or restricting the distribution, of computers incorporating x86 CPUs supplied by Advanced Micro Devices (AMD), Intel's only serious competitor[8]. The General Court also confirmed Commission's understanding that both

4. It is wrong to consider the *Guidance* a set of guidelines on the law of Article 102. The document is what it says it is: guidance on the Commission's enforcement priorities. In the EU competition law system, the EU Courts have the prerogative to determine what is and what is not an abuse of dominant position. The Commission can define priorities of enforcement and expect to influence future development of jurisprudence of the EU Courts, but cannot contradict established case-law.
5. Case T-286/09 *Intel Corp.* v *Commission* [2014], not yet published. An appeal by Intel against the judgment is pending before the Court of Justice (Case C-413/14 P *Intel Corporation* v *Commission*).
6. OJ [2009] C 227.
7. Owner of the retail chain Media Markt, a major retailer of microelectronics devices in Europe.
8. Several manufacturers of x86 CPUs had exited the market in the years before 2000. After that, Intel and AMD became the only companies still manufacturing x86 CPUs (*Intel* judgment, para 22).

abuses constituted a single strategy aimed at foreclosing AMD implemented from October 2002 to December 2007.

The *Intel* judgment addressed several relevant topics related to the legal assessment of exclusivity rebates under Article 102. In essence, the judgment avoided any significant movement towards a less formal approach to that category of rebates, explicitly rejecting the need for demonstration of anticompetitive effects for a finding of abuse[9], for the reason that exclusivity rebates inherently restrict customers' freedom to choose their own suppliers and rivals' access to such customers when adopted by dominant companies[10].

The judgment treated topics already addressed in precedents of the EU Courts (e.g. the need for demonstration of actual foreclosure effects[11] or for evidence of binding written agreement[12]) and also some novel points, such as the relevance of the 'as-efficient competitor' analysis for the legal assessment of conditional rebates[13] or the application of 'exclusivity' when only a segment of the relevant market is affected[14].

Although Intel's appeal is still pending[15], full understanding of the legal standards set forth in the *Intel* judgment is indispensable for mapping the main parameters that should guide undertakings concerned about the application of Article 102 to rebate practices. Inspired by such intent, this book discusses the standards for legal assessment of exclusivity rebates stated in the *Intel* judgment.

Section 2 below provides a brief overview of the Commission's decision and the General Court's judgment. Section 3 dissects the legal assessment of exclusivity rebates made by the General Court in order to identify and criticize the legal standards adopted in the judgment. Section 4 comments on the main practical implications of the *Intel* judgment, including for the surrounding debate concerning the role of the *Guidance on Enforcement Priorities* to the assessment of exclusionary conduct in general and exclusivity rebates in particular. Section 5 concludes.

9. *Ibid.*, paras 77 and 86.
10. *Ibid.*, para 77.
11. *Ibid.*, paras 86 and 103.
12. *Ibid.*, para 106.
13. *Ibid.*, paras 149-153.
14. *Ibid.*, paras 129-132.
15. See note 5 above.

2

The *Intel* case and the General Court judgment

The Commission imposed a fine of €1.06 billion (the largest ever imposed on a single firm at that time) on Intel for having abused its dominant position in the worldwide market for x86 CPUs, from October 2002 to October 2007, by means of a strategy aimed at foreclosing AMD from the market. CPUs are a key component of any computer and are generally divided into two categories: x86 CPUs and CPUs based on another instruction set architecture. The x86 architecture is a standard designed by Intel for its CPUs, which started with 8086 in the late seventies and was followed by many successors ending in "86", such as 80386 and 80486 processors. This architecture was also adopted by Intel's competitors, including AMD[16].

According to the Commission's decision, the abuse consisted of several measures implemented with certain computer manufacturers and one retailer of microelectronic devices, which were divided in two group of practices, each of them sufficient to constitute an individual abuse under Article 102[17]: (i) exclusivity rebates and (ii) naked restrictions. The assessment of the naked restrictions is not object of this book.

16. See OJ [2009] C 227/07, paras 14-15.
17. *Ibid.*, paras 21 and 40: "The Decision describes two types of Intel conduct vis-à-vis its trading partners: conditional rebates and so-called naked restrictions. (...) The Decision establishes that each of the Intel conducts vis-à-vis individual OEMs mentioned above and vis-à-vis MSH constitutes an abuse of Article [102 TFEU], but that these individual abuses are also part of a single strategy aimed at foreclosing AMD, Intel's only significant competitor, from the market for x86 CPUs. The individual abuses are therefore part of a single infringement of Article [102]".

The Commission found that Intel's dominant position derived from its significant market share (around 70%) and the high barriers to entering and expanding in the market (mainly unrecoverable investments in research and development, production facilities and intellectual property)[18]. In addition, Intel was understood to be an unavoidable supplier of x86 CPUs since customers would inevitably obtain part of their requirements from it (must-stock products)[19].

The Commission concluded that the exclusivity rebates significantly diminished the ability of Intel's competitors to compete on the merits in the market for x86 CPUs, resulting in a reduction of consumer choice and in lower incentives for innovation[20].

The General Court upheld the Commission's decision *in totum*. The main topics of the Intel judgment (from the perspective of the present book) are summarised below.

Categorisation. The General Court understood that the rebates Intel granted to Dell, HP, NEC and Lenovo and the payments to MSH pertain to the category of 'exclusivity rebates', the legal treatment of which is not identical to those for 'loyalty-inducing rebates' or 'quantity rebates'[21].

Anticompetitive nature. Exclusivity rebates by dominant companies will typically infringe Article 102, except if they are objectively justified, as

18. The Commission did not establish whether there is a single x86 CPU market for all computers or whether it is necessary to distinguish between three distinct x86 CPU markets (desktop computers, notebook computers and servers). Considering Intel's market share for each segment, the Commission found that there is no difference to the conclusion of dominance. See OJ [2009] C 227/07, paras 16-20.
19. *Ibid.*, para 19.
20. *Ibid.*, para 33.
21. *Intel* judgment, para 76: "there are rebates the grant of which is conditional on the customer's obtaining all or most of its requirements from the undertaking in a dominant position. That type of rebate, to which the Commission refers by the expression 'fidelity rebates within the meaning of Hoffmann-La Roche', will subsequently be referred to as 'exclusivity rebates'. It should be noted that that expression will also be used for rebates which are not conditional on exclusive supply but on the customer's obtaining most of its requirements from the undertaking in a dominant position".

they restrict buyers' freedom to choose the source of supply and deny other suppliers access to the market[22].

Analysis of circumstances of the case and demonstration of actual effects. The corollaries of the inherent anticompetitive nature of exclusivity rebates by dominant undertakings are that there is no need to carry out a case-specific analysis of circumstances[23] nor to show actual effects of the rebates on competition[24]. Consequently, the demonstration of causal

22. *Ibid.*, para 77: "Such exclusivity rebates, when applied by an undertaking in a dominant position, are incompatible with the objective of undistorted competition within the common market, because they are not based — save in exceptional circumstances — on an economic transaction which justifies this burden or benefit but are designed to remove or restrict the purchaser's freedom to choose his sources of supply and to deny other producers access to the market [...]. Such rebates are designed, through the grant of a financial advantage, to prevent customers from obtaining their supplies from competing producers".
23. *Ibid.*, paras 80-93, particularly: "84. It follows that, according to the case-law, it is only in the case of rebates falling within the third category that it is necessary to assess all the circumstances, and not in the case of exclusivity rebates falling within the second category. 85. That approach can be justified by the fact that exclusivity rebates granted by an undertaking in a dominant position are by their very nature capable of restricting competition. 86. The capability of tying customers to the undertaking in a dominant position is inherent in exclusivity rebates. The grant by an undertaking in a dominant position of a rebate in consideration of a customer's obtaining all or most of its requirements implies that the undertaking in a dominant position grants a financial advantage designed to prevent customers from obtaining their supplies from competing producers. It is therefore not necessary to examine the circumstances of the case in order to determine whether that rebate is designed to prevent customers from obtaining their supplies from competitors. 87. It should moreover be noted that exclusivity rebates granted by an undertaking in a dominant position are by their very nature capable of foreclosing competitors. A financial advantage granted for the purpose of inducing a customer to obtain all or most of its requirements from the undertaking in a dominant position means that that customer has an incentive not to obtain, in respect of the part of its requirements concerned by the exclusivity condition, supplies from competitors of the undertaking in a dominant position".
24. *Ibid.*, para 103: "First of all, it must be stated that, even in the context of an analysis of the circumstances of the case, the Commission must only show that a practice is capable of restricting competition [...]. The mechanism of an exclusivity rebate granted by an undertaking in a dominant position which is an unavoidable trading partner enables it to use the non-contestable share of the demand of the customer as leverage to secure also the contestable share (see paragraph 93 above). When

link between those effects and the exclusivity rebates, direct damage to consumers, or causal link between such damage and the exclusivity rebates is also superfluous[25].

'As-efficient competitor' test. It is also entirely unnecessary for the Commission to conduct an economic analysis of the capability of the rebates to foreclose a hypothetical competitor that is as efficient as the dominant undertaking[26].

Conditional nature. Even where there is no written agreement and customers' purchasing decisions may be influenced by multiple factors (such as quality, reliability, availability etc.), evidence that a discount is linked to exclusivity is sufficient to establish the conditional nature of the rebate[27]. The level of the rebate, the inexistence of proof that it was the main reason for the customers' purchasing behaviour and the fact that the customers themselves might have proposed the exclusivity condition were all considered irrelevant[28].

---

such a trading instrument exists, it is unnecessary to undertake an analysis of the actual effects of the rebates on competition".

25. *Ibid.*, paras 104-105.
26. *Ibid.*, paras 143-146.
27. *Ibid.*, para 543: "The Court finds that, by providing an alternative explanation for the existence of an exclusive relationship between the applicant and Dell, the applicant does not call in question the fact that the level of the MCP rebates was conditional upon exclusivity. Even supposing that the applicant succeeded in proving that Dell used the applicant as its exclusive supplier solely for the reasons put forward by the applicant, that would not call into question the probative value of the evidence on which the Commission relied in order to establish the existence of an exclusivity rebate. The evidence put forward by the applicant would be capable only of disproving the causal link between the exclusivity rebate, the existence of which was proved to the requisite legal standard in the contested decision, and Dell's decision to use the applicant as its exclusive supplier. However, that evidence would not be capable of disproving the existence of an exclusivity rebate as such".
28. *Ibid.*, paras 108-109: "108. However, as the Commission correctly observes, it is not the level of the rebates which is at issue in the contested decision but the exclusivity for which they were given. Thus, the rebate must only be capable of inducing the customer to purchase exclusively, irrespective whether the competing supplier could have compensated the customer for the loss of the rebate if that customer switched supplier. 109. It is not therefore necessary to consider the question whether, in the purely theoretical example of a rebate in an amount of USD 1 only

Exclusivity even if only a market segment is covered. The exclusive condition will infringe Article 102 even if it accounts for only a segment of the relevant product market, regardless of the fact that this segment represents a small part of the customer's total demand[29].

Market coverage. In addition, the possible smallness of the part of market concerned is irrelevant, since there is no 'appreciable effect' criterion or *de minimis* threshold for a finding of infringement of Article 102[30]. Anyway, a coverage of approximately 14% of the relevant market was considered 'significant'[31].

Duration. Alleged short duration of contracts or the possibility of termination at short notice does not eliminate competition concerns[32].

---

as put forward by the applicant, such a minimum rebate is capable of constituting an incentive for the customer to comply with the exclusivity condition. In the case in point, the Commission proved to the requisite legal standard that the applicant had granted rebates to the OEMs amounting to millions of USD annually. The Commission moreover proved to the requisite legal standard that those rebates were granted, at least in part, in consideration of exclusivity [...]. Those matters suffice to show that the exclusivity rebates at issue in the contested decision were capable of inducing the OEMs to purchase exclusively".

29. *Ibid.*, paras 129 and 132.
30. *Ibid.*, para 116: "In addition, the possible smallness of the parts of the market which are concerned by the practices at issue is not a relevant argument. Where the course of conduct under consideration is that of an undertaking occupying a dominant position on a market where for this reason the structure of competition has already been weakened, any further weakening of the structure of competition may constitute an abuse of a dominant position [...]. The Court of Justice has therefore rejected the application of an 'appreciable effect' criterion or a de minimis threshold for the purposes of applying Article [102 TFEU] (Opinion of Advocate General Mazák in Case C-549/10 P Tomra, [...], point 17)".
31. *Ibid.*, para 194: "In the present case, the expert report that the applicant provided as an annex to the reply and which bears the reference C.1 indicates, in paragraph 48, that the share of the global market concerned by the conduct described in the contested decision was approximately 14% on average during the total period of the infringement found by the Commission, if the calculation is not limited to only the contestable share of the demand of the customers concerned. The Court is of the view that such a share must be regarded as significant".
32. *Ibid.*, para 111: "That argument must also be rejected. In that regard, it must be borne in mind that, in principle, any financial incentive to purchase exclusively constitutes additional interference with the structure of competition on a market

Furthermore, a one-year term is not short[33] and, in any event, the applicable standard is the total period during which the dominant company adopted exclusivity rebates[34].

Objective justification. Exclusivity rebates by dominant undertakings will not be abusive if based on admissible justification, in particular the demonstration that the practice "is objectively necessary or that the potential foreclosure effect that it brings about may be counterbalanced, outweighed even, by advantages in terms of efficiency that also benefit consumers"[35]. The argument that the exclusivity rebates were a request by customers or a response to their buyer power is not an admissible justification for that purpose[36].

and must therefore be regarded as abusive to the extent that it is implemented by an undertaking in a dominant position".

33. *Ibid.*, para 113: "Moreover, it should be noted that, in the present case, for all the OEMs and for MSH, the total period during which exclusivity rebates were applied was not short. That period lasted from approximately one year, in the case of Lenovo, to more than five years, in the case of MSH. In that context, it must be stated that the incentive for customers to purchase all or almost all of their requirements from the undertaking in a dominant position continues to exist for as long as the latter grants exclusivity rebates, irrespective of whether a long-term contract has been concluded or whether there is a succession of several short-term contracts".
34. *Ibid.*, para 195: "With respect, next, to the applicant's argument that its supply contracts were only of short duration or that they could be terminated at 30 days' notice, it should be noted that the relevant criterion is not the duration of the notice period for terminating a contract or the fixed duration of an individual contract which forms part of a series of successive contracts, but the overall period during which the applicant applies exclusivity rebates and payments vis-à-vis a customer (see paragraphs 112 and 113 [of the Judgment]). In the present case, that period amounted to approximately five years in the case of MSH, approximately three years in the case of Dell and NEC, more than two years in the case of HP and approximately one year in the case of Lenovo. The grant of exclusivity rebates and payments during such periods is generally capable of restricting competition. That holds especially true in relation to a market such as the CPU market, which is characterised by a high level of dynamism and short product-life cycles".
35. *Ibid.*, para 94.
36. *Ibid.*, para 139: "That argument must be rejected. The claim – even if it were established – that the rebates granted by the applicant represented a response to requests and to customers' buying power does not justify making them subject to an exclusive supply condition [...]. As the Court of Justice held in Hoffmann-La

Intel's appeal pending before the Court of Justice[37] discusses almost all of the topics above. It claims that the General Court applied the wrong legal standard to assess the legality of its conduct, since it erred in law by:

(i) concluding that the rebates in question were inherently capable of restricting competition;

(ii) assessing the capability to restrict competition "on the basis of abstract considerations rather than likely or actual effects"; and

(iii) disregarding "a number of relevant factors that should have been considered, such as the market coverage of the practice, the duration of the alleged practices, actual market evidence of rapidly declining prices and a lack of foreclosure, and the conclusions to be properly drawn from the as-efficient competitor test carried out by the Commission during the administrative proceeding".

Intel also claims that the General Court erred in (i) finding an infringement for the final two years of the alleged period of infringement, given that the respective market coverage in that period was, at most, 3.5% of the relevant market; and (ii) classifying as 'exclusivity rebates' the practice with HP and Lenovo, as it concerned no more than 28% and 42% of each customer's total purchases of the relevant product. Other grounds of appeal address extraterritorial jurisdiction and the level of the fine, among other issues.

Roche [...], the fact that the dominant undertaking's contracting partner is itself a powerful undertaking and that the contract is clearly not the outcome of pressure brought to bear by the dominant undertaking on its partner does not preclude the existence of an abuse of a dominant position, since such an abuse consists in the additional interference, due to the obligation to obtain supplies exclusively, with the structure of competition in a market in which in consequence of the presence there of an undertaking occupying a dominant position the degree of competition has already been weakened. Moreover, the OEMs' buying power does not alter the fact that they depended on the applicant as an unavoidable trading partner in the x86 CPU market".

37. Case C-413/14 P *Intel Corporation* v *Commission*.

3

Legal standards for assessment of exclusivity rebates – discussion of the General Court's approach

Each of the main elements of the assessment of exclusivity rebates in the *Intel* judgment is examined below. When relevant, the analysis also traces its roots and pinpoints its location in the broader context of academic debate.

3.1 Categorisation of rebates

Since *Hoffmann-La Roche*[38], EU Courts have developed a basic distinction between loyalty rebates (also called fidelity rebates) and quantity rebates. Loyalty rebates were generally understood as those "granted in return for an undertaking by the customer to obtain his stock exclusively or almost exclusively from an undertaking in a dominant position"[39], independently of whether the quantities purchased were large or small. Quantity rebates were understood as those "exclusively linked with the volume of purchase from the producer concerned"[40].

Thus, the notion of loyalty rebates under EU case-law was closely associated with the idea of exclusivity, which is to some extent more restrictive than is the notion of loyalty rebates usually adopted in other

38. Case 85/76 *Hoffmann-La Roche* v *Commission* [1979] ECR 461 ('*Hoffmann-La Roche*').
39. Case T-203/01 *Michelin* v *Commission* [2003] ECR II-04071 ('*Michelin II*'), para 56.
40. *Hoffmann-La Roche*, para 90.

jurisdictions – typically understood as discounts or rebates on units of a single product purchased, conditional upon the level or share of purchases[41].

In its *Guidance on Enforcement Priorities*, the European Commission avoided the distinction between loyalty (or exclusivity) and quantity rebates, preferring a distinction between conditional and unconditional rebates. Conditional rebates were defined as "rebates granted to customers to reward them for a particular form of purchasing behaviour", usually "if [their] purchases over a defined reference period exceed a certain threshold, the rebate being granted either on all purchases (retroactive rebates) or only on those made in excess of those required to achieve the threshold (incremental rebates)"[42].

In the *Intel* judgment, however, the General Court identified three categories of rebates[43]:

(i) quantity rebates: non-retroactive rebate systems linked solely to the volume of purchases;

(ii) exclusivity rebates: those directly conditional to the customer's obtaining all or most of its requirements from the undertaking in a dominant position – which is equivalent to the traditional definition of loyalty rebates noted above; and

(iii) 'third category' rebates (or 'loyalty-inducing' rebates): rebate systems not directly linked to a condition of exclusive or quasi-exclusive supply, but whereby the mechanism for granting may also have a fidelity-building effect – such as those in *Michelin I*[44], *British Airways*[45] and *Tomra*[46]. They comprise rebate mechanisms conditional to achievement of individual sales objectives,

41. See ICN's Unilateral Conduct Working Group, *Report on the Analysis of Loyalty Discounts and Rebates under Unilateral Conduct Laws* (2009), available at www.internationalcompetitionnetwork.org/uploads/library/doc357.pdf, p. 4.

42. *Guidance*, para 37.

43. *Intel* judgment, paras 74-78.

44. Case 322/81 *Nederlandsche Banden Industrie Michelin* v *Commission* [1983] ECR 3461('*Michelin I*').

45. Case C-95/04 P *British Airways* v *Commission* [2007] ECR I-2331 ('*British Airways*').

46. Case C-549/10 P *Tomra Systems and Others* v *Commission* [2012] ECR ('*Tomra*').

where such objectives do not consist of obtaining all or a given proportion of supplies from the dominant undertaking[47].

Quantity rebates are presumptively lawful under Article 102, since they are deemed to reflect gains in efficiency and economies of scale made by the dominant undertaking[48].

Exclusivity rebates are presumptively unlawful when adopted by dominant undertakings and will only be admitted if objectively justified, according to the General Court[49].

By contrast, the legality or illegality of 'third category' ('loyalty-inducing') rebates is not presumed *prima facie*. It depends on detailed analysis considering all circumstances, particularly the criteria and mechanisms ruling the granting of rebates and the existence of objective justification. If the advantage offered is not economically justified, the illegality of the rebate scheme will depend on whether it "tends to remove or restrict the buyer's freedom to choose his sources of supply, to bar competitors from access to the market, or to strengthen the dominant position by distorting competition"[50].

47. *Intel* judgment, para 78.
48. *Michelin II*, para 58: "Quantity rebate systems linked solely to the volume of purchases made from an undertaking occupying a dominant position are generally considered not to have the foreclosure effect prohibited by Article [102 TFEU] (see Michelin v Commission, [...], paragraph 71, and Case C-163/99 Portugal v Commission [2001] ECR I-2613, paragraph 50). If increasing the quantity supplied results in lower costs for the supplier, the latter is entitled to pass on that reduction to the customer in the form of a more favourable tariff (Opinion of Advocate General Mischo in Portugal v Commission, [...], at ECR I-2618, point 106). Quantity rebates are therefore deemed to reflect gains in efficiency and economies of scale made by the undertaking in a dominant position".
49. *Intel* judgment, para 76: "Second, there are rebates the grant of which is conditional on the customer's obtaining all or most of its requirements from the undertaking in a dominant position. That type of rebate, to which the Commission refers by the expression 'fidelity rebates within the meaning of Hoffmann-La Roche', will subsequently be referred to as 'exclusivity rebates'. It should be noted that that expression will also be used for rebates which are not conditional on exclusive supply but on the customer's obtaining most of its requirements from the undertaking in a dominant position".
50. *Michelin I*, para 73: "In deciding whether Michelin NV abused its dominant position in applying its discount system it is therefore necessary to consider all the circumstances, particularly the criteria and rules for the grant of the discount, and to investigate whether, in providing an advantage not based on any economic

According to the General Court, the rebates granted by Intel to Dell, HP, NEC and Lenovo, as well as the payments to MSH fall within the category of 'exclusivity rebates'[51].

The categorisation adopted by the General Court in *Intel* has been criticised by some authors as artificial or too formalistic[52]. However, there does not seem to be a serious problem with the typology of rebates delineated in the judgment. On the contrary, the didactic organisation of the multiple rebate practices according to three categories, and the prompt identification of the legal treatment applicable to each, is commendable, at least as an example of clarity in judicial discourse[53]. The settled case-law of EU Courts on the matter lacked an appropriate classification of the different types of rebates that was informative of the discipline of the practice under Article 102. Moreover, the value of such kind of categorisations depends on whether they are legally and economically sound as well as able to establish

---

service justifying it, the discount tends to remove or restrict the buyer's freedom to choose his sources of supply, to bar competitors from access to the market, to apply dissimilar conditions to equivalent transactions with other trading parties or to strengthen the dominant position by distorting competition". See also *British Airways*, para 67; and *Tomra*, para 71.

51. *Intel* judgment, paras 79 ("The rebates granted to Dell, HP, NEC and Lenovo to which the Commission referred, in particular in Article 1(a) to (d) of the contested decision, are rebates falling within the second category, namely exclusivity rebates. According to the Commission's findings set out in the contested decision, those rebates were conditional upon customers' purchasing from Intel, at least in a certain segment, either all their x86 CPU requirements, in the case of Dell and Lenovo, or most of their requirements, namely 95% in the case of HP and 80% in the case of NEC.") and 167 ("The Commission finds in essence, at recital 1000 of the contested decision, that the effect of the payments granted to MSH on condition that it sell exclusively the applicant's products was equivalent to that of an exclusivity rebate and that those payments therefore fulfilled the conditions laid down by the case-law for qualification as abusive").
52. See, for instance, D. Geradin, "Loyalty Rebates after Intel: Time for the European Court of Justice to Overrule *Hoffman-La Roche*" (2015) 11 Journal of Competition Law & Economics, pp. 21-22; and J. Venit, "Case T-286/09 *Intel* v *Commission* – The Judgment of the General Court: All Steps Backward and No Steps Forward" (2014) 10 European Competition Journal 2, p. 211.
53. See N. Petit, "*Intel*, Leveraging Rebates and the Goals of Article 102 TFEU" (2015) available at ssrn.com/abstract=2567628, p. 5.

a clear and coherent distinction of the legal treatment among categories[54] – as the General Court seems to have done in *Intel.*

3.2 Anticompetitive nature of exclusivity rebates

One of the most contentious aspects of the *Intel* judgment is the steady reaffirmation of the formal (or 'form-based') approach under Article 102 to rebates conditioned on exclusivity.

The General Court made it very clear that exclusivity rebates, when adopted by an undertaking in a dominant position, are by their very nature capable of restricting competition[55], thus endorsing the settled case-law since *Hoffmann-La Roche*[56].

a) Reasoning

The main line of reasoning to justify the approach is the inherent capacity of the exclusivity rebates to restrict competition by means of limiting customers' freedom to choose suppliers and rivals' access to such customers[57]. According to the General Court, a harm to competition occurs by the granting of a rebate in consideration of customers' obtaining

54. M. Adam and F. Maier-Rigaud, "The Law and Economics of Article 82 EC and the Commission Guidance Paper on Exclusionary Conduct" (2011) Journal of Competition Law (ZWeR - Zeitschrift für Wettbewerbsrecht), 2009, 1, 131-146, pp. 138-139.
55. *Intel* judgment, para 85: "That approach can be justified by the fact that exclusivity rebates granted by an undertaking in a dominant position are by their very nature capable of restricting competition".
56. *Hoffmann-La Roche*, para 90: "Obligations of this kind to obtain supplies exclusively from a particular undertaking [...] are incompatible with the objective of undistorted competition within the common market, because [...] they are not based on an economic transaction which justifies this burden or benefit but are designed to deprive the purchaser of or restrict his possible choices of sources of supply and to deny other producers access to the market". See also Case T-155/06 *Tomra Systems and Others* v *Commission* [2010] ECR II-4361, para 209.
57. *Intel* judgment, para 77: "Such exclusivity rebates, when applied by an undertaking in a dominant position, are incompatible with the objective of undistorted competition within the common market, because they are not based — save in exceptional circumstances — on an economic transaction which justifies this burden or benefit but are designed to remove or restrict the purchaser's freedom to choose his sources of supply and to deny other producers access to the market

all or most of their requirements from the dominant undertaking, since it consists of giving a financial benefit designed to prevent customers from obtaining their supplies from competitors[58].

The notion of the inherent anticompetitive nature of exclusivity rebates under Article 102 is also based on two important associated ideas.

First, according to EU case-law[59], an anticompetitive result under Article 102 occurs even when access to the market is made more difficult for competitors, and not exclusively when such access is made impossible[60]. The reason is that the very existence of dominance (or 'substantial market power', a better expression) by one of the players in the market – in other words, the very presence of an undertaking that, by definition, has the ability to act "independently of its competitors, customers and ultimately of its consumers"[61] – implies that competition is already distorted in that market[62], with the result that additional restriction to competition in such a context should not be tolerated without convincing justification.

[...]. Such rebates are designed, through the grant of a financial advantage, to prevent customers from obtaining their supplies from competing producers".

58. *Ibid.*, para 86: "The capability of tying customers to the undertaking in a dominant position is inherent in exclusivity rebates. The grant by an undertaking in a dominant position of a rebate in consideration of a customer's obtaining all or most of its requirements implies that the undertaking in a dominant position grants a financial advantage designed to prevent customers from obtaining their supplies from competing producers. It is therefore not necessary to examine the circumstances of the case in order to determine whether that rebate is designed to prevent customers from obtaining their supplies from competitors".
59. *Michelin I*, para 85; *Michelin II*, para 244; Case C-52/09 *TeliaSonera Sverige* [2011] ECR I-527 ('*TeliaSonera*'), para 63.
60. *Intel* judgment, para 88: "In that context, it should be observed that a foreclosure effect occurs not only where access to the market is made impossible for competitors, but also where that access is made more difficult [...]. A financial incentive granted by an undertaking in a dominant position in order to induce a customer not to obtain, in respect of the part of its requirements concerned by the exclusivity condition, supplies from its competitors is by its very nature capable of making access to the market more difficult for those competitors".
61. Case 27/76 *United Brands* v *Commission* [1987] ECR 207 ('*United Brands*'), para 65.
62. *Intel* judgment, para 89; Case C-310/93 P *BPB Industries and British Gypsum* v *Commission* [1995] ECR I-865, para 11.

Second, it follows that a dominant undertaking has a special responsibility not to permit its conduct to "impair genuine undistorted competition"[63]. In this regard, exclusive supply conditions by an undertaking in a dominant position cause additional interference with the structure of competition in the market, thus constituting unacceptable obstacle to accessing the market if not objectively justified[64].

In parallel, the General Court adduced an additional line of reasoning for the anticompetitive nature of exclusivity rebates that is based on arguments of structural nature: "the grant of an exclusivity rebate by an unavoidable trading partner makes it structurally more difficult for a competitor to submit an offer at an attractive price and gain access to the market"[65].

In this regard, the Court stated that (i) generally, the supplier in a dominant position is, to a large extent, an unavoidable trading partner, and (ii) in the case in question, Intel can be considered as holding the position of an unavoidable trading partner, since it occupies a 'strong dominant position' and did not contest the findings made in the Commission's decision that, for a substantial part of the demand, there are no proper substitutes for the product it supplies[66].

63. *Intel* judgment, para 90: "That approach is justified by the special responsibility that an undertaking in a dominant position has not to allow its conduct to impair genuine undistorted competition in the common market and by the fact that, where an economic operator holds a strong position in the market, exclusive supply conditions in respect of a substantial proportion of purchases by a customer constitute an unacceptable obstacle to access to the market [...]. In that case, the exclusivity of supply causes additional interference with the structure of competition on the market. Thus, the concept of abuse in principle includes any obligation to obtain supplies exclusively from an undertaking in a dominant position which benefits that undertaking". See also Case T-65/89 *BPB Industries and British Gypsum* v *Commission* [1993] ECR II-389, paras 65-68.
64. *Michelin I*, para 57: "It is not possible to uphold the objections made against those arguments by Michelin NV, supported on this point by the French Government, that Michelin NV is thus penalized for the quality of its products and services. A finding that an undertaking has a dominant position is not in itself a recrimination but simply means that, irrespective of the reasons for which it has such a dominant position, the undertaking concerned has a special responsibility not to allow its conduct to impair genuine undistorted competition on the common market".
65. *Intel* judgment, para 93.
66. *Ibid.*, para 91: "Furthermore, it must also be stated that it is inherent in a strong dominant position, such as that occupied by the applicant, that, for a substantial

The Court pointed that if an unavoidable supplier exists, the remaining competitors cannot compete for the full supply of a customer, but only for a portion of its demand ('the contestable share'), as customers will in any case acquire part of their requirements from the dominant 'unavoidable' supplier ('the non-contestable share')[67]. Consequently, the granting of exclusivity rebates enables the dominant undertaking to use its economic power in the non-contestable share of the demand as leverage to capture the contestable share, thus making access to the market structurally more difficult for a competitor, since it will necessarily have to offer to customers some sort of compensation for the loss they will incur by losing the entire exclusivity rebate[68]. In other words, it will not be sufficient for competitors

part of the demand, there are no proper substitutes for the product supplied by the dominant undertaking. The supplier in a dominant position is thus, to a large extent, an unavoidable trading partner".

67. *Ibid.*, para 92: "It follows from the position of unavoidable trading partner that customers will in any event obtain part of their requirements from the undertaking in a dominant position ('the non-contestable share'). The competitor of an undertaking in a dominant position is not therefore in a position to compete for the full supply of a customer, but only for the portion of the demand exceeding the non-contestable share ('the contestable share'). The contestable share is thus the portion of a customer's requirements which can realistically be switched to a competitor of the undertaking in a dominant position in any given period, as the Commission states at recital 1009 of the contested decision. The grant of exclusivity rebates by an undertaking in a dominant position makes it more difficult for a competitor to supply its own goods to customers of that dominant undertaking. If a customer of the undertaking in a dominant position obtains supplies from a competitor by failing to comply with the exclusivity or quasi-exclusivity condition, it risks losing not only the rebates for the units that it switched to that competitor, but the entire exclusivity rebate".
68. *Ibid.*, para 93: "In order to submit an attractive offer, it is not therefore sufficient for the competitor of an undertaking in a dominant position to offer attractive conditions for the units that that competitor can itself supply to the customer; it must also offer that customer compensation for the loss of the exclusivity rebate. In order to submit an attractive offer, the competitor must therefore apportion the rebate that the undertaking in a dominant position grants in respect of all or almost all of the customer's requirements, including the non-contestable share, to the contestable share alone. Thus, the grant of an exclusivity rebate by an unavoidable trading partner makes it structurally more difficult for a competitor to submit an offer at an attractive price and thus gain access to the market. The grant of exclusivity rebates enables the undertaking in a dominant position to use its economic power on the non-contestable share of the demand of the customer

to offer attractive conditions for only the units comprising the contestable share of the customer's demand – which means that access to the market is made more difficult to some extent.

Although it is based on the notion of 'leverage from the non-contestable share of demand to capture part of the contestable one', the structural line of reasoning in the *Intel* judgment does not essentially transcend the formal approach to exclusivity rebates adopted therein, as the General Court unequivocally states that there is no need for a quantitative analysis of resulting anticompetitive effects.

Curiously, such structural argumentation is essentially the basis of the approach presented in the *Guidance on Enforcement Priorities* in the context of a detailed, quantitative assessment of effects on competition resulting from conditional rebates[69], praised by most of the critics of the traditional, formal approach to exclusivity rebates.

Nevertheless, the fact that the structural arguments is used to support the quantitative analysis of actual foreclosure effects and the 'as-efficient competitor' test in the *Guidance* does not, in itself, invalidate its adoption as one of the reasons that justify the view of the anticompetitive nature of exclusivity rebates in the context of a formal approach, as adopted in the *Intel* judgment. The structural line of reasoning does not contradict – as some authors argue[70] – the other reasoning related to the inherent capacity of restricting customers' freedom of choice and competitors' access to market resulting from exclusivity rebates by dominant undertakings. Instead, they reinforce each other. Exclusivity rebates by a dominant undertaking makes access to the market more difficult for competitors (thus infringing the special responsibility imposed by Article 102 to that undertaking) either by restricting customers' freedom to choose suppliers and rivals' access to those customers as well as by making the submission of attractive offers by competitors structurally more difficult (when the dominant undertaking is also an unavoidable trading partner).

Another point to remark is that the explicit connection made by the Court between the notions of 'strong dominant position' and 'unavoidable

as leverage to secure also the contestable share, thus making access to the market more difficult for a competitor".

69. *Guidance*, paras 39-44.

70. Geradin, *supra* note 52, p. 24.

trading partner' in paragraph 91 might raise doubts, at first glance, about whether the condition of 'unavoidable trading partner' is an attribute of a special category of the dominant undertakings: those that hold a qualified 'strong' dominant position, different from supposed 'ordinary' dominant position. In the case of Intel, the 'strong' dominant position appears to be linked to its consistently high market share (around 70%) and the formidable barriers to entry and expansion during the relevant period.

However, a careful reading of the judgment reveals that the Court did not establish that the condition of 'unavoidable trading partner' depends on the undertaking holding a 'strong dominant position'. The qualification of Intel's position as 'strongly dominant' appears to be merely an aspect that contributes to supporting the presumption that Intel was, in fact, an unavoidable trading partner during the relevant period. There is no solid basis to sustain that, in this case, the General Court constructed a special category of dominant undertakings to which it would be possible to ascribe the condition of unavoidable trading partner.

The Court did not expressly indicate which of the two lines of reasoning above prevails[71]. It seems that the two approaches are complementary: the structural arguments (focused on the 'non-contestable *v* contestable' shares of the market), as discussed above, reinforce the elucidation of why exclusivity rebates adopted by a dominant undertaking (by inherently restricting customers' freedom of choice and limiting rivals' access to such customers) makes access to the market more difficult for a competitor – a conduct that will only be admitted under Article 102 if not objectively justified.

b) 'Form-based' approach

Typically, a formal (or 'form-based') approach under competition law involves the legal presumption that conduct pertaining to a certain

71. Petit argues that the General Court would have limited the application of the presumption of illegality (referred to as "modified per se prohibition rule") to "a narrow subset of exclusivity rebates, ie leveraging rebates" (Petit, *supra* note 53). However, nothing in the *Intel* judgment appears to support the view that the legal treatment established for exclusivity rebates should be applied narrowly as encompassing only the situation in which a dominant undertaking seeks to leverage the non-contestable share of a given customer's demand to capture a greater share of the contestable share of that demand.

pre-defined category is, by its very nature, 'harmful to competition' (also said 'capable of restricting competition' or even 'incompatible with the objectives of competition law'), irrespective of any case-specific quantitative analysis of actual or potential market effects[72]. In this sense, the General Court approach to exclusivity rebates in *Intel* is essentially 'form-based', as it considers such rebates as capable of restricting competition by their very nature when adopted by a dominant undertaking.

The origin of the 'form-based' terminology in EU competition law dates back to the 1990s, in the context of the debate surrounding the reform of the block exemption regulations for vertical agreements (now under Article 101(3) TFEU)[73].

Critics of the settled case-law concerning exclusivity rebates commonly refer to the 'form-based' approach as fundamentally undesirable and unsound from both the legal and the economic perspective[74]. Critics also say that the 'form-based' approach is not based on effects, since an 'effects-based' approach (also referred to as 'more economic approach') – which was already adopted in the modernisation of Article 101[75] and

72. According to ICN, "[the formalistic, bright-line] approach tends to be based on the presumption that a particular conduct leads to anticompetitive or procompetitive effects. It allows little or no room for an agency or court to take into account the actual market effects of the prohibited conduct in the particular circumstances". See ICN, *Unilateral Conduct Workbook - Chapter 1: The Objectives and Principles of Unilateral Conduct Laws* (2012), available at www.internationalcompetitionnetwork.org/uploads/library/doc827.pdf, p. 11.
73. See R. Whish, "Regulation 2790/99: The Commission's 'New Style' Block Exemption for Vertical Agreements" (2000) 37 CMLR 887. One of the main criticism of the block exemption regulations in force between 1967 and 2000 was their formalistic exemption rules with no market share caps, resulting that, for instance, exclusive purchasing agreements were exempted regardless of the market power of the undertakings concerned. The reform (Commission Regulation (EC) No 2790/1999 of 22 December 1999 on the application of Article 81(3) of the Treaty to categories of vertical agreements and concerted practices, OJ [1999] L 336) corrected this deficiency by introducing a market share cap of 30%.
74. See, for instance, R. O'Donoghue and J. Padilla, *The Law and Economics of Article 102 TFEU* (Hart, 2013), p. 267.
75. In 1996, the Commission initiated a long campaign to reform the interpretation and application of Article 101 TFEU with the view that consumer welfare should be the benchmark to assess agreements, based on an economic-oriented and less rigid analysis of anticompetitive effects. The reform of the block exemption

of the EC Merger Regulation[76] – typically involves case-specific, detailed (and often complex) assessment of actual or potential effects on market conditions[77].

The 'effect-based' (or 'more economic') approach to Article 102 was presented as the ultimate goal of a review process of interpretation and application of Article 102 announced in 2005 by the then Competition Commissioner, Neelie Kroes[78]. Its intellectual foundation can be traced back in the report of June 2005 by the Economic Advisory Group on Competition Policy (EAGCP)[79], which advocated an 'economics-based' approach to Article 102 "in a way similar to the reform of Article 81 and merger control", focused "on the presence of anti-competitive effects that harm consumers"[80]. In December 2005, the Commission released the *DG Competition discussion paper on the application of Article [102] of the Treaty to exclusionary abuses*[81] for public consultation, which resulted in the *Guidance on Enforcement Priorities.*

The *Guidance* establishes that the Commission will typically intervene against exclusionary conduct by dominant undertakings only if it

regulation (mentioned in note 73 above) was one of the main steps of this process. For details, see A. Jones, "Left Behind by Modernisation? Restrictions by Object under Article 101(1)" (2011) 649 European Competition Journal 2010.

76. On May 1, 2004, the new EU Merger Regulation introduced significant substantive and procedural modifications to the merger rules. Commission Regulation 139/2004 OJ [2004] L 24/1.
77. For a critical and contextual overview of the discussion of the relevance of case-specific effect analysis to assess conduct under Article 102 as well as the role of the *Guidance* in the expected development of case-law, see R. Whish and D. Bailey, *Competition Law* (Oxford University Press, 2015) pp. 183-187.
78. N. Kroes, "Preliminary Thoughts on Policy Review of Article 82", Speech at the Fordham Corporate Law Institute, New York, 23 September 2005, available at www.europa.eu/rapid/press-release_SPEECH-05-537_en.htm.
79. EAGCP, report: "An economic approach to Article 82" (2005) available at ec.europa.eu/dgs/competition/economist/eagcp_july_21_05.pdf
80. According to the EAGCP's report, "[a]n economics-based approach to the application of article [102] implies that the assessment of each specific case will not be undertaken on the basis of the form that a particular business practice takes (for example, exclusive dealing, tying, etc.) but rather will be based on the assessment of the anti-competitive effects generated by business behavior" (ibid, p. 3).
81. Available at www.ec.europa.eu/competition/antitrust/art82/discpaper2005.pdf.

is likely to result, based on cogent and convincing evidence, in foreclosure leading to harm to consumers (called 'anticompetitive foreclosure')[82]. In this regard, the *Guidance* is unequivocal that the foreclosure leading to harm to consumers is the one that "[has] an adverse impact on consumer welfare"[83].

Specifically regarding the category of 'price-based exclusionary conduct', the *Guidance* defines the 'as-efficient competitor' test as the standard for intervention by the Commission[84]. The *Guidance* also makes it clear that the 'as-efficient competitor' test is the standard for intervention against conditional rebates, which are included in the general category of 'price-based exclusionary conduct'. According to the Guidance, when applying the methodology of the 'as-efficient competitor' analysis, "the Commission intends to investigate, to the extent that the data are available and reliable, whether the rebate system is capable of hindering expansion or entry even by competitors that are equally efficient by making it more difficult for them to supply part of the requirements of individual customers" [85].

It thus becomes clear that the proposed outcome of the current criticism of the formal approach is quite different to the one of the criticism

82. *Guidance*, para 20.
83. *Ibid.*, para 19: "The aim of the Commission's enforcement activity in relation to exclusionary conduct is to ensure that dominant undertakings do not impair effective competition by foreclosing their competitors in an anti-competitive way, thus having an adverse impact on consumer welfare, whether in the form of higher price levels than would have otherwise prevailed or in some other form such as limiting quality or reducing consumer choice. In this document the term 'anti-competitive foreclosure' is used to describe a situation where effective access of actual or potential competitors to supplies or markets is hampered or eliminated as a result of the conduct of the dominant undertaking whereby the dominant undertaking is likely to be in a position to profitably increase prices to the detriment of consumers. The identification of likely consumer harm can rely on qualitative and, where possible and appropriate, quantitative evidence. The Commission will address such anti-competitive foreclosure either at the intermediate level or at the level of final consumers, or at both levels".
84. *Ibid.*, para 23: "With a view to preventing anti-competitive foreclosure, the Commission will normally only intervene where the conduct concerned has already been or is capable of hampering competition from competitors which are considered to be as efficient as the dominant undertaking".
85. *Ibid.*, para 41.

at the time the 'form-based' terminology emerged. While a 'less-formal' approach in the present discussion of abusive conducts tends to diminish the emphasis on the distinct effects of dominant and non-dominant undertakings' conduct, the 'less-formal' approach proposed in the 1990s[86] implied more rigorous treatment of undertakings with market power by excluding them from the benefits of the block exemptions.

Although the *Guidance* clearly states that it is not intended to constitute a test for assessing whether exclusionary conduct violates Article 102 TFEU (a statement of the law, or a 'legality test'), but just a test to be used by the Commission to define whether or not a case would be a priority for enforcement (a 'prioritisation test')[87], many critics of the settled case-law have expected that the prioritisation test proposed in the *Guidance* would be adopted by the EU Courts as the new 'legality test' for exclusionary conduct in general, and for exclusivity rebates in particular[88].

86. See note 73 above.
87. *Guidance*, paras 2 and 3: "2. This document sets out the enforcement priorities that will guide the Commission's action in applying Article [102] to exclusionary conduct by dominant undertakings. Alongside the Commission's specific enforcement decisions, it is intended to provide greater clarity and predictability as regards the general framework of analysis which the Commission employs in determining whether it should pursue cases concerning various forms of exclusionary conduct and to help undertakings better assess whether certain behaviour is likely to result in intervention by the Commission under Article [102]. 3. This document is not intended to constitute a statement of the law and is without prejudice to the interpretation of Article [102] by the Court of Justice or the [General Court] of the European Communities. In addition, the general framework set out in this document applies without prejudice to the possibility for the Commission to reject a complaint when it considers that a case lacks priority on grounds of lack of Community interest".
88. See, for instance, O'Donoghue and Padilla, *supra* note 74, pp. 67-93 and 471-508; D. Geradin, "A Proposed Test for Separating Pro-Competitive Conditional Rebates from Anti-Competitive Ones" (2008) available at ssrn.com/abstract=1315292; D. Geradin and C. Pereira Neto, "For a Rigorous 'Effects-Based' Analysis of Vertical Restraints Adopted by Dominant Firms: An Analysis of the EU and Brazilian Competition Law" (2012) available at ssrn.com/abstract=2173735; and G. Federico, "The Antitrust Treatment of Loyalty Discounts in Europe: Towards a more Economic Approach" (2011) 2 JECLAP 3; H. Zenger, "Loyalty Rebates and the Competitive Process" (2012) 8 Journal of Competition Law & Economics 4.

b.1) Legal perspective of the 'form-based' approach

From the legal perspective, the criticism of the 'form-based' approach seems unconvincing.

The label 'form-based' is frequently used to qualify an approach as undesirable or somewhat superficial. However, the process of classification of conducts or conditions into distinct categories, followed by the attribution of a corresponding 'legality test' for them, is inherent to the mechanics of law itself.

For instance, in EU competition law, it is none other than a 'form-based' rule that establishes that only undertakings in a condition of dominance (substantial market power) can infringe Article 102, or that prices below a certain level of costs, irrespective of any evidence of the intent to eliminate competitors, will be considered a predatory pricing abuse[89].

The wording of the prohibition of abuse of dominance in Article 102 is vague. Consequently, it is impossible to legally interpret and apply it without the use of categories, and therefore 'form-based' rules.

In addition, the proper interpretation of Article 102 must render the prohibition of abuses of dominance administrable[90]. Not only the officials and judges that have to apply it, but also dominant undertakings (the potential violators) as well as their competitors, clients and business partners (the potential direct victims) must be able to assess and predict, in advance, at reasonable cost and with reasonable certainty, whether the practice at hand is lawful or not under Article 102.

Another unconvincing criticism of the 'form-based' approach to exclusivity rebates is that it would entail 'per se' illegality of discount

89. In *AKZO*, the Court of Justice made it clear that a predatory pricing abuse will exist whenever the Commission (or a claimant) is able to show that the prices charged by the dominant undertaking are below average variable costs, being unnecessary to show that the strategy is likely to amount to foreclosure or that the undertaking would be in a position to recoup its losses (Case C-62/86 *AKZO Chemie BV* v *Commission* [1991] ECR I-3359, para 71). See also Case C-202/07 P *France Télécom* v *Commission* [2009] ECR I-2369, paras 109-111.

90. See W. Wils, "The judgment of the EU General Court in *Intel* and the so-called 'more economic approach' to abuse of dominance" (2014) 37 World Competition: Law and Economics Review 4, p. 20.

practices, which would be detrimental to consumers because they are, at the outset, deprived of accessing products at lower costs. In essence, the 'form-based' approach is different from the mere 'per se' illegality as it still allows the investigated undertaking to put forward justifications and defences that may outweigh actual or potential negative effects on competition derived from the conduct. In the case of 'per se' illegality, no justification or defence is allowed, as the conduct represents, in itself (or 'per se'), a violation of law[91].

In summary, the 'form-based' approach under Article 102 does not determine the illegality of conduct, as the dominant undertaking will always have right to show that the exclusivity is justified by convincing efficiencies or an objective necessity. In this scenario, the Commission would then have the burden of showing why the justification is not acceptable[92].

For this reason, it is not correct to state that the *Intel* judgment imposes a 'per se' approach to exclusivity rebates. As seen, the legal presumption of illegality – applied only when the undertaking is dominant – has the effect of reversing the burden of proof to the undertaking to demonstrate that conditioning of rebates on exclusivity is objectively justified. This is not materially different from the application rule of Article 101 TFEU: whenever an agreement is found to infringe (by its object or effects) Article 101(1), the burden is then on the parties to the agreement to produce evidence that the agreement leads to economic efficiencies according to Article 101(3).

In this sense, the legal discipline adopted in *Intel* for exclusivity rebates is very similar to the one for restrictions of competition 'by object' under Article 101: with respect precisely to agreements between undertakings that, *by their very nature*, are capable of restricting competition (or "harmful to the proper functioning of normal competition")[93], the application of Article

91. See R. Whish, "*Intel* v *Commission*: Keep Calm and Carry on!" (2015) 6 JECLAP 1, pp. 1-2. See also A. Italianer, "The Object of Effects" (2014) Speech at Charles River Associates Conference, Brussels, 10 December 2014, available at ec.europa.eu/competition/speeches/text/sp2014_07_en.pdf, p. 4.

92. See section 3.10 below.

93. Case C-226/11 *Expedia* v *Autorité de la concurrence* [2012] ECR ("*Expedia*"), paras 35-36. See also Case C-209/07 *Beef Industry Development Society and Barry Brothers* [2008] ECR I-8637, para 17; and Case C-8/08 *T-Mobile Netherlands and Others* [2009] ECR I-4529, para 29.

101(1) does not depend on any specific demonstration of actual or likely effects on the market[94]. To all other agreements, there is no presumption that they are caught by Article 101(1), and individual assessment of its likely effects on competition is required (with the Commission bearing the burden of proof). In both cases, the parties to the agreement are not precluded from demonstrating that the practice is individually justified by efficiencies under Article 101(3).

Likewise, with regard to exclusivity rebates, the General Court decided that when they are adopted by a dominant undertaking, they are *by their very nature* capable of restricting competition (since they inherently restricts customers' freedom to choose sources of supply, thus making access to the market more difficult). Consequently, it is not legally necessary to examine the circumstances of the case to determine whether, for the purposes of Article 102, those rebates are capable of restricting competition. In any case, as mentioned, it is open to the dominant undertaking to demonstrate that the conduct is individually justified by efficiencies or other objective reasons[95].

Terminologically, the words "object or effects" are present in Article 101, but not in Article 102. However, as seen, they only reflects the idea that practices caught by Article 101 can be divided into those that are harmful to competition 'by nature' and those that will only harm competition in particular circumstances. And it does not seem wrong or inappropriate – from legal and economic standpoints[96] – to adopt the same dichotomy in the legal discipline of Article 102.

Thus, a conduct that, when adopted by a dominant undertaking, is by its very nature capable of restricting competition constitutes an *abuse* under Article 102 unless it is objectively justified. If the conduct is not inherently capable of restricting competition, however, the *abuse* will only exist if (i) a case-specific analysis of circumstance reveals its capacity to restrict competition and (ii) there is no objective justification for it.

94. See, to that effect, Joined Cases 56/64 and 58/64 *Consten and Grundig* v *Commission* [1966] ECR 299.

95. See section 3.10 below.

96. See discussion of economic perspective below.

The fact that exclusivity agreements do not constitute a restriction of competition 'by object' for the purposes of Article 101[97] is not incompatible with the understanding that exclusivity rebates not objectively justified would be an *abuse of dominant position* under Article 102. As seen, the very presence of a dominant undertaking means that the state of the competition in that market is already distorted. In addition, the discipline of Article 102, differently from that of Article 101, includes the principle of special responsibility of the dominant undertaking, which imposes to that undertaking the duty not to allow its conduct to cause additional distortion to the structure of competition of that market. In this sense, the understanding that exclusivity rebates – and, logically, exclusive dealing arrangements without rebates – are by their very nature capable of restricting competition for the purposes of Article 102 is perfectly compatible with the view that, for the purposes of Article 101, exclusivity agreements do not have the object of restricting competition[98].

Thus, in summary, the 'form-based' approach adopted by the General Court consists of the legality test establishing that exclusivity rebates adopted by dominant companies constitute an abuse under Article 102 unless objectively justified, since:

(i) the state of competition in a market with the presence of a dominant undertaking is already distorted;

(ii) the dominant undertaking has special responsibility of not allowing its conduct to cause additional distortion to competition in that market;

(iii) an exclusivity rebate scheme by a dominant undertaking is capable, by its nature, of causing additional distortion to competition (by tying customers to the dominant supplier, and therefore restricting customers' freedom of choice and rivals' access to market); and

(iv) in parallel, when it is granted by an unavoidable trading partner, such rebates also make it structurally more difficult for a competitor to submit an attractive offer (and thus gain access to the market).

97. Case C-234/89 *Delimitis* v *Henninger Brau* [1991] ECR I-935, paras 14-27.

98. See Whish, *supra* note 91, pp. 1-2; Italianer, *supra* note 91, p. 4.

Therefore, from the legal perspective, a 'form-based' rule concerning exclusivity rebates by dominant undertakings does not, in principle, seem undesirable or unsound. As discussed above, law typically involves categories and formal rules, the application of which must be administrable, especially when they entail direct prohibition subject to public and private enforcement and are formulated in vague wording (as is Article 102). In addition, a formal rule is not, in itself, determinative of illegality, as the dominant undertaking always has the possibility of adducing evidence that the conduct is objectively justified under Article 102.

b.2) Economic perspective of the 'form-based' approach

From the economic perspective, the 'form-based' approach is criticised as being economically unsound and old-fashioned[99]. Such criticism usually comes in the form of allegations that the 'form-based' approach is 'less economic' – and, on the other hand, that the so-called 'effects-based' approach is more aligned with 'current economic teaching'. The implicit proposition is that the settled case-law on exclusivity rebates does not reflect consistent economic thinking.

This is not exactly true. The interpretation and application of Article 102 TFEU, as of any other major aspect of competition law, necessarily requires economic thinking. There is no doubt that the authors of the 1957 Treaty establishing the European Economic Community, the judges who erected the settled case-law and now the members of the General Court who reaffirmed it based their reasoning on economic considerations to support their respective views and positions[100]. Therefore, the argument that the approach of the General Court to exclusivity does not reflects economic thinking or is 'less economic' seems fragile[101].

99. See Geradin, *supra* note 52; P. Rey and J. Venit, "An Effects-Based Approach to Article 102: A Response to Wouter Wils" (2015) 38 World Competition.

100. P. Behrens, "The Ordoliberal Concept of 'Abuse' of a Dominant Position and its Impact on Article 102 TFEU" (2015) Nihoul/Takahashi, Abuse Regulation in Competition Law, Proceedings of the 10th ASCOLA Conference Tokyo 2015, available at ssrn.com/abstract=2658045, pp. 2-8.

101. It would be unnecessary to say that, contrary to what the expression 'more economic approach' suggests, the use of economics in the interpretation and application of Article 102 TFEU should not be assessed as a matter of quantity,

It is clear that the discussion at this point refers to the distinct theories of economic competition, and the associated different theories of harm to competition process resulting from exclusivity rebates by dominant companies.

As with any social science, economic science encompasses a range of possible approaches and schools of thought[102]. The advocates of the aforementioned 'effects-based' approach to exclusivity rebates embrace one specific economic theory of competition: the consumer welfarist approach[103], which values the competitive process to the extent that it delivers positive results in terms of consumer welfare (or efficiency), making the application of competition law rules dependent on a case-specific assessment of the effects of the conduct on consumer welfare[104].

However, although widespread and close to being conventional wisdom today, the consumer welfarist approach is far from being the only possible economic approach to abusive conducts by dominant undertakings.

Other consistent economic theories examine the competitive market mechanism (or the competition process) from a different, broader perspective, emphasising the benefits of a system of undistorted competition that protects the individual economic freedom of market participants as an independent value, favouring the range of choice (variety and consumer

but in consideration of its consistency and adequacy with the purposes for which it is intended.

102. See Wils, *supra* note 90, p. 11: "[t]he adherence by an economist to one or another approach or school, or the relative popularity of one or another approach or school in a certain group of economists or at a certain point in time is not the result of a process of falsification, the other approaches having been proved wrong. It rather reflects a preference for a way of looking at things that is found congenial or instrumentally useful for some task at hand, or, when the approach becomes conventional wisdom, loyalty to the tribe, possibly re-enforced through peer review and other mechanisms of professional discipline".

103. Also referred to as the Chicago or post-Chicago consumer welfarist approach.

104. Illustrating that the 'consumer welfare' is at the centre of the so-called 'effects-based' approach proposed in the Commission's *Guidance*, see press release IP/08/1877, 'Antitrust: consumer welfare at heart of Commission fight against abuses by dominant undertakings' (3 December 2008), available at: europa.eu/rapid/press-release_IP-08-1877_en.htm?locale=en.

choice)[105], the right to compete on the merits, and equality of opportunity for economic operators[106].

In fact, if the meaning of allocative efficiency is satisfaction of consumers' preferences, then it is reasonable to propose that consumers' preferences are to be revealed by market transactions based on consumers' choice. In this sense, Friedrich Hayek's proposition "to consider competition systematically as a procedure for discovering facts which, if the procedure did not exist, would remain unknown or at least would not be used" leads to the conclusion that "competition is important only because and insofar as its outcomes are unpredictable and on the whole different from those that anyone would have been able to consciously strive for"[107].

For a similar view, see Amartya Sen's examination of the competitive market mechanism from the perspective of individual freedom, emphasising not only its opportunity aspects (maximal achievement and range of choice) but also its process aspect (decisional autonomy and immunity from interference)[108].

According to such views, exclusivity clearly constitutes a distinct source of harm to competition process, as it inherently restricts customers' economic freedom (to choose suppliers), thus restricting the residual competition that remains in a market in which the state of competition is already distorted by the presence of a dominant undertaking. This perspective is not dissonant with the view that economic freedom is one

105. Although the 'consumer welfarist' approach does not ignore the relevance of the range of choice for consumers, the excessive focus on price and cost results in such aspects frequently being neglected in practice. See, for instance, the discussion on the application of the 'as-efficient competitor' test to exclusivity rebates in section 3.5 below. See also B. Orbach's discussion that "under all present interpretations of the term 'consumer welfare', there are several sets of circumstances in which the application of antitrust laws may hurt consumers and reduce total social welfare" (B. Orbach, "The Antitrust Consumer Welfare Paradox" (2011) 7 Journal of Competition Law & Economics 1).

106. See Wils, *supra* note 90, pp. 11-13. See also Behrens, *supra* note 100, pp. 14-20'.

107. F. Hayek, "Competition as a Discovery Procedure" (2002) 5 The Quarterly Journal of Austrian Economics 3, pp. 9-10.

108. A. Sen, "Markets and Freedoms: Achievements and Limitations of the Market Mechanism in Promoting Individual Freedoms" (1993) 45 Oxford Economic Papers 4, pp. 519-541.

of the multiple goals of EU competition law[109], together (and sometimes in conflict[110]) with the consumer welfare goal, and with particular relevance in the interpretation and application of Article 102.

In this sense, as summarized by Behrens, "[i]f competition is seen as a dynamic system of interaction of producers and consumers making choices between different lines of production and different sources of supply respectively, then it follows that abuse must be understood to refer to a restriction of market participants' freedom to make such choices which in turn is determined by the market structure. (...) Hence, 'abuse' in Article 102 TFEU refers to an improper restriction of the residual competition that remains in an already concentrated market where one or some firms hold, individually or collectively, a dominant position"[111].

The approach adopted by the General Court in *Intel* is unequivocal regarding the understanding that exclusivity constitutes a distinct source of harm to competition process. As mentioned above, the anticompetitive nature of exclusivity rebates by Intel was due to its inherent "capability of tying customers" and the fact that "the grant of an exclusivity rebate by an unavoidable trading partner makes it structurally more difficult for a competitor to submit an offer at an attractive price and thus gain access to the market"[112].

According to the General Court, "the present case does not relate to a pricing practice. As regards the rebates granted to the various OEMs, the complaint made against the applicant in the contested decision is not based on the exact amount of the rebates and thus on the prices charged by the applicant, but on the fact that the grant of such rebates was conditional

109. See G. Monti, *EC Competition Law* (Cambridge University Press, 2007), pp. 20-52; L. Gormsen, *A Principled Approach to Abuse of Dominance in European Competition Law* (Cambridge University Press, 2010); P. Nihoul, "The Ruling of the General Court in *Intel*: Towards the End of an Effect-based Approach in European Competition Law?" (2014) JECLAP first published online September 15, 2014; Behrens, *supra* note 100.

110. See L. Gormsen, "The Conflict between Economic Freedom and Consumer Welfare in the Modernisation of Article 82 EC" (2007) 3 European Competition Journal 2. See also O. Andriychuk, "Rediscovering the Spirit of Competition: On the Normative Value of the Competitive Process" (2011) 6 European Competition Journal 3.

111. Behrens, *supra* note 100, p. 16.

112. *Intel* judgment, para 93.

on exclusive or quasi-exclusive supply. Different treatment of exclusivity rebates and pricing practices is justified by the fact that, unlike an exclusive supply incentive, the level of a price cannot be regarded as unlawful in itself"[113].

On the other hand, under a consumer welfarist approach such as the one adopted in the *Guidance on Enforcement Priorities*, exclusivity rebates will normally be assessed as 'price-based exclusionary conduct'. Accordingly, an exclusivity rebate system will only be considered harmful to the competition process as long as it is capable of excluding competitors as efficient as the dominant company from the market, since the source of harm would ultimately be the low level of prices[114], and not the inherent restriction to customers' freedom of choice and rivals' access to the market resulting from exclusivity. In addition, it is arguable that the price offered in exchange for exclusivity would necessarily be lower than the price that the dominant undertaking would charge in the absence of the exclusivity rebate system[115].

113. *Ibid.*, para 99: "However, the scope of that case-law is limited to pricing practices and does not affect the legal characterisation of exclusivity rebates. Case C-280/08 P Deutsche Telekom, paragraph 98 above, and TeliaSonera, paragraph 88 above, concerned margin squeeze practices and Post Danmark, paragraph 94 above, concerned low price practices, so that those three cases concerned pricing practices. However, the present case does not relate to a pricing practice. As regards the rebates granted to the various OEMs, the complaint made against the applicant in the contested decision is not based on the exact amount of the rebates and thus on the prices charged by the applicant, but on the fact that the grant of those rebates was conditional on exclusive or quasi-exclusive supply. Different treatment of exclusivity rebates and pricing practices is justified by the fact that, unlike an exclusive supply incentive, the level of a price cannot be regarded as unlawful in itself".

114. See *Guidance*, para 25: "In order to determine whether even a hypothetical competitor as efficient as the dominant undertaking would be likely to be foreclosed by the conduct in question, the Commission will examine economic data relating to cost and sales prices, and in particular whether the dominant undertaking is engaging in below-cost pricing. This will require that sufficiently reliable data be available. Where available, the Commission will use information on the costs of the dominant undertaking itself. If reliable information on those costs is not available, the Commission may decide to use the cost data of competitors or other comparable reliable data".

115. See N. Economides, 'Tying, Bundling and Loyalty/Requirement Rebates' in *Research Handbook on the Economics of Antitrust Law*, ed. E. Elhauge (Edward

According to this perspective, the approach to exclusivity rebates adopted in the *Intel* judgment appears to be economically more consistent and sounder than the one proposed by the self-labelled 'more economic' or 'effects-based' approach, considering that the essence of the problem in *Intel* was the exclusivity, not the price.

Moreover, according to the *Intel* judgment, the reason for the prohibition of the use of unjustifiable exclusivity rebates by dominant undertakings is indeed their restrictive effects on customers' freedom to choose suppliers and competitors' possibility to supply those customers, thus creating an additional distortion in the process of competition in a market which it is already distorted by the very presence of a dominant undertaking. From this angle, one cannot deny that the *Intel* judgment is, in this particular way, 'based on effects'[116].

It is relevant to remember that, although the wording of Article 102 is somewhat vague, leaving some space for different interpretations, any possible interpretation must – in order to be admissible – be compatible with the rules, principles and statements of purpose contained in the EU Treaties. Considering that the EU Treaties clearly establish that the objective of Article 102 TFEU is a system of undistorted competition as part of the internal market[117-118], the General Court's approach in *Intel* is not dissonant with that goal.

Elgar, 2012), pp. 121 and 130-131; E. Elhauge, "How Loyalty Discounts Can Perversely Discourage Discounting" (2009) 5 Journal of Competition Law & Economics 1.

116. See Wils, *supra* note 90, pp. 23-24.

117. TFEU states in Article 3(3) as one of its goals the establishment of an "internal market". Protocol No 27 on the "internal market and competition", annexed to and with the same legal force as TFEU, explains that the "internal market" includes "a system ensuring that competition is not distorted" (OJ [2010] C 83/309).

118. See *TeliaSonera*, paras 20-22: "20. In order to answer those questions, it must be observed at the outset that Article 3(3) TEU states that the European Union is to establish an internal market, which, in accordance with Protocol No 27 on the internal market and competition, annexed to the Treaty of Lisbon (OJ 2010 C 83, p. 309), is to include a system ensuring that competition is not distorted. 21. Article 102 TFEU is one of the competition rules referred to in Article 3(1)(b) TFEU which are necessary for the functioning of that internal market. 22. The function of those rules is precisely to prevent competition from being distorted to the detriment of the public interest, individual undertakings and consumers,

Therefore, from the economic perspective, although the *Intel* judgment is not aligned with (today's) predominant economic theory of competition and delivered the opposite result to what expected by the advocates of the so-called 'effects-based' or 'more economic' approach, it seems a sensible decision even on economic grounds, as it correctly identifies exclusivity as a different and more appropriate source of harm than low prices as far as exclusivity rebates by dominant undertakings are concerned.

3.3 No need for analysis of the circumstances of the case

The first practical consequence of the definition of the inherent anticompetitive nature of exclusivity rebates under Article 102 is the absence of any need for a case-specific analysis of circumstance to establish the capacity to produce restrictive effects on competition.

As explained above, according to the General Court's approach, exclusivity itself constitutes a distinctive source of harm (negative *effects*) to competition, which is derived from its inherent restriction to customers' freedom of choice and rivals' access to the market.

In a market where the very existence of a dominant operator means that the state of the competition is already distorted and, consequently, such operator has a special responsibility to avoid its conduct to cause additional distortion to competition, it is not necessary to analyse the circumstances of the case to conclude that an exclusivity rebate practice by the dominant undertaking produces additional distortive effects on competition. Therefore, the effective ability of the rebate practice to lead to the so-called 'anticompetitive foreclosure'[119] is beyond the requisite legal standard for assessment of exclusivity rebates under Article 102[120].

thereby ensuring the well-being of the European Union (see, to that effect, Case C-94/00 Roquette Frères [2002] ECR I-9011, paragraph 42)". See also Case C-496/09 *Commission* v *Italy* [2011] ECR I-11483, para 60.

119. See section 3.1 above.

120. *Intel* judgment, para 143: "First of all, it should be recalled that a finding that an exclusivity rebate is illegal does not necessitate an examination of the circumstances of the case (see paragraphs 80 to 93 [of the judgment]). The Commission is not therefore required to demonstrate the foreclosure capability of exclusivity rebates on a case-by-case basis".

The Court acknowledged that case-specific analysis of circumstances is only needed when the rebate system falls within the 'loyalty-inducing' category, as previously affirmed by case-law[121]. It also stated that, even in the context of the analysis of case-specific circumstances concerning 'loyalty-inducing' rebates, it is only necessary for the requisite legal standard to demonstrate that the practice is capable of restricting competition[122], which is understood as the capacity to remove or restrict the buyer's freedom to choose his sources of supply, to bar competitors from access to the market, or to strengthen the dominant position by distorting competition[123]. In summary, the illegality of 'loyalty-inducing' rebates does not depend on the demonstration of foreclosure leading to harm to consumers (the so-called 'anticompetitive foreclosure' of the Commission's *Guidance*)[124].

3.4 No need for demonstration of actual effects

Another important practical consequence of the anticompetitive nature of exclusivity rebates by dominant undertakings is that it is completely irrelevant for the assessment of legality under Article 102 the analysis of actual foreclosure effects, even if the conduct has been in place for a sufficient period.

In this regard, Intel claimed that, during the period covered by the contested decision, AMD reaped great commercial success[125].

121. *Ibid.*, paras 96-97. See also *Michelin I*; *British Airways.*

122. *Ibid.*, para 103: "First of all, it must be stated that, even in the context of an analysis of the circumstances of the case, the Commission must only show that a practice is capable of restricting competition [...]. The mechanism of an exclusivity rebate granted by an undertaking in a dominant position which is an unavoidable trading partner enables it to use the non-contestable share of the demand of the customer as leverage to secure also the contestable share (see paragraph 93 [of the judgment]). When such a trading instrument exists, it is unnecessary to undertake an analysis of the actual effects of the rebates on competition [...]".

123. *Michelin I*, para 73; *British Airways*, para 67; and *Tomra*, para 71.

124. *Guidance*, para 20.

125. See *Intel* judgment, para 185: "First, the applicant attempts to demonstrate that its practices were not capable of restricting competition by arguing that, during the relevant period, AMD reaped the greatest commercial success in its history, reported uniquely rapid growth rates with the very OEMs deemed to be the target of abusive behaviour, faced manufacturing capacity constraints that hampered its ability to satisfy demand for its CPUs and grew its investments in research and

However, as mentioned above, the requisite legal standard for assessment of rebate systems under Article 102 is the demonstration that the practice is capable of restricting competition. As also seen above, the capability of restricting competition is inherent in exclusivity rebates when adopted by dominant companies. Thus, the fact that such 'capability of restricting competition' has not produced, in practice, any apparent negative effect on the competition process does not prevent the application of Article 102.

Citing *British Airways126*, the General Court affirmed that whenever a dominant undertaking adopts practices capable of restricting competition, the fact that it does not produce actual effects is not sufficient to avoid the application of Article 102. The Court added that it may legitimately be considered that, in the absence of those practices, the increase in the competitor's market share and the decrease in the price of the relevant product (as alleged in *Intel*) might have been greater, and it would thus be incorrect to state that the practices had no negative effects[127].

development. Moreover, the quality-adjusted price of CPUs fell 36.1% annually over the period covered by the contested decision".

126. Case T-219/99 *British Airways* v *Commission* [2003] ECR II-5917, para 297.

127. *Intel* judgment, para 186: "Those arguments cannot be accepted. Where an undertaking in a dominant position actually puts into operation practices which are capable of restricting competition, the fact that that capability does not produce actual effects cannot suffice to prevent the application of Article [102 TFEU] (see, to that effect, Case T-219/99 British Airways v Commission [2003] ECR II-5917, paragraph 297). The fact that, over the period covered by the contested decision, AMD reaped great commercial success and, consequently, faced capacity constraints could at most show that the applicant's practices did not produce actual effects. However, that could not suffice to demonstrate that the practices implemented by the applicant were not capable of restricting competition. Moreover, neither the growth in the market shares of AMD and in its research and development investment, nor the decrease in the price of x86 CPUs over the period covered by the contested decision mean that the applicant's practices had no effect. In the absence of those practices, it may legitimately be considered that the increase in the competitor's market share and in its research and development investment and the decrease in the price of x86 CPUs might have been greater (see, to that effect, Michelin II, [...], paragraph 245, and British Airways v Commission, paragraph 298). Consequently, it is not necessary to adjudicate on the Commission's assertions that the applicant's arguments concerning the increase in AMD's market shares and the decrease in the price of x86 CPUs are factually incorrect".

In summary, according to the *Intel* judgment, even when the envisioned conduct has been in place for a sufficient period, there is no need to demonstrate actual effects on the market or direct harm to consumers. As a logical result, there is also no need to demonstrate causal link between the practice and such effects or harm.

It also follows also that Intel's claims that customers purchased from it on an exclusive basis for business reasons completely independent of the rebates, even if proved, does not preclude the illegality of the conduct under Article 102 because, as stated by the Court, it "does not mean that those rebates were not capable of inducing customers to obtain their supplies exclusively from it"[128].

3.5 Irrelevance of the as-efficient competitor test

One of the main arguments submitted by Intel against Commission's decision was that the 'as-efficient competitor' (AEC) analysis would be part of the legality test under Article 102 even in the case of exclusivity rebates and, as such, this analysis would be crucial for establishing potential anticompetitive effects (said to be the likelihood of foreclosure leading to consumer harm)[129]. Intel argued that the AEC analysis conducted by the Commission failed to establish the foreclosure capability of the investigated conduct.

The AEC analysis carried out by the Commission in *Intel* was an economic examination intended to determine the price at which a competitor as efficient as Intel would have had to offer the product to compensate a customer for the loss of a rebate granted by Intel[130]. However, when so doing, the Commission expressly stated that the AEC analysis was not part of the legality assessment of the conduct[131].

128. *Ibid.*, para 104.

129. See section 3.2 above.

130. See Commission's decision, paras 1002-1575.

131. According to the Commission, although the *Guidance* was inapplicable to *Intel* (as the proceeding was initiated before its adoption), it decided to include a 150-pages long AEC analysis to show that the decision was in line with the orientations established in the *Guidance*.

As seen above, the Commission's *Guidance* adopted the AEC analysis as the standard for defining priorities of enforcement by the Commission (prioritisation test) regarding 'price-based exclusionary conduct', a category in which the *Guidance* included exclusivity rebates[132]. As explained above, the *Guidance* defines as the standard for intervention the capability of the conduct concerned of "hampering competition from competitors which are considered to be as efficient as the dominant undertaking", which will be determined by examination of "economic data relating to cost and sales prices, and in particular whether the dominant undertaking is engaging in below-cost pricing". Based on this analysis, in principle the Commission will not intervene "if the data clearly suggest that an equally efficient competitor can compete effectively with the pricing conduct of the dominant undertaking"[133].

The General Court refuted Intel's argument on several grounds[134]. First, as seen above, legal assessment of exclusivity rebates under Article 102 does not require examination of the circumstances on a case-by-case basis. Second, even when it is necessary (e.g. 'loyalty-inducing' rebates), examination of specific circumstances does not require carrying out the AEC test (i.e. quantitative demonstration that competitors had been forced to sell at a loss to compensate for the rebates)[135]. Third, the finding of effects detrimental to competition does not involve showing that a competitor as efficient as the dominant undertaking is forced to charge below-cost prices by the rebate system, but only showing the existence of a loyalty mechanism[136] (which, as seen, is considered inherent to exclusivity rebates).

In addition, the Court emphasised that a foreclosure effect occurs not only when access to the market is made impossible for competitors, but also where it is made more difficult. This means that whether the Commission carried out the AEC test in accordance with the applicable rules is completely irrelevant, since the AEC test only verifies the hypothesis that access to the market by competitors has been made impossible.

132. See text accompanying note 85 above.

133. *Guidance*, paras 23-27.

134. *Intel* judgment, paras 143-147.

135. *Michelin I*, paras 81-86.

136. *Tomra*, paras 73-74 and 79.

Nevertheless, the General Court's position is neither a complete rejection of the price-and-cost analysis in general (and of the AEC analysis in particular) to assess conduct under Article 102, nor a refusal of the practical relevance of the Commission's *Guidance*.

The EU Courts have already acknowledged the relevance of the AEC test in particular and of the quantitative analyses of foreclosure effects in general to the legal assessment of other types of infringements of Article 102 – see *TeliaSonera*, *Deutsche Telekom*[137] and *Post Danmark*[138].

The fundamental difference between those cases and *Intel* (as well as *Tomra*, *British Airways*, *Michelin II*, *Michelin I* and *Hoffmann La-Roche*) is that the former involved truly price-based practices (i.e. margin squeeze and selective low prices), while the latter involved exclusivity and loyalty-inducing rebates, in which case the source of harm to competition is the problem of exclusivity (or the fidelity-inducing mechanism)[139].

As underlined by the General Court, the obligation to carry out detailed price-and-cost (as well as AEC) analyses is due to the impossibility of assessing "whether a price is abusive without comparing it with other prices and costs. A price cannot be unlawful in itself"[140]. On the other hand, when it comes to exclusivity rebates by dominant undertakings, it is the condition of exclusivity that makes them anticompetitive, not the amount of the rebate offered or the price level of a potentially attractive offer by a competitor.

In the same sense, the Commissioner of US Federal Trade Commission J. Wright argues that exclusive dealing framework is superior to price-cost standards for the legal assessment of loyalty discounts and other forms of partial exclusives such as market-share discounts and shelf space share contracts, as it is a legal test that "moves the legal and economic analyses of the underlying conduct closer together rather than further apart", differently from the predatory pricing framework[141].

137. Case C-280/08 P *Deutsche Telekom* v *Commission* [2010] ECR I-9555.

138. Case C-209/10 *Post Danmark* [2012] ECR.

139. See section 3.2 above.

140. *Intel* judgment, para 152.

141. J. Wright, "Simple but Wrong or Complex but More Accurate? The Case for an Exclusive Dealing-Based Approach to Evaluating Loyalty Discounts" (2013) Speech at Bates White 10th Annual Antitrust Conference, Washington, DC, 3 June

With regard to the *Guidance*, since it is nothing more than guidance on the standards for selecting cases for enforcement (priorities) to be used by the Commission[142], the *Intel* judgment does not affect its validity and applicability[143].

In fact, the Commission has already indicated that it will immediately apply the legal test set out by the General Court to exclusivity rebates as well as to exclusive dealings[144], even if an appeal against the judgment is pending, and that it will also continue to apply the effects-based approach (i) to legally evaluate other types of abuses in which the EU Courts have already endorsed a legal test based on the appreciation of effects (such as margin squeeze or selective low prices, as noted above) and (ii) to select priority cases for enforcement with regard to exclusivity rebates and exclusive dealing conducts[145]. Considering that the Commission initiated *Intel* and *Tomra* before the adoption of the *Guidance*, it is pointless to question whether the Commission observed the standards of the *Guidance* in those cases[146].

2013, available ftc.gov/sites/default/files/documents/public_statements/simple-wrong-or-complex-more-accurate-case-exclusive-dealing-based-approach-evaluating-loyalty/130603bateswhite.pdf, p. 33. See also S. Gates, "Antitrust by Analogy: Developing Rules for Loyalty Rebates and Bundled Discounts" (2013) 79 Antitrust Law Journal.

142. See section 2 above.

143. For a discussion of discretion and prioritisation in the enforcement of Articles 101 and 102 by the European Commission, see W. Wils, "Discretion and Prioritisation in Public Antitrust Enforcement, in Particular EU Antitrust Enforcement" (2011) 34 World Competition: Law and Economics Review 3.

144. This is logical, since if exclusivity rebates by dominant undertakings are by their very nature distortive of competition, the same must be true of exclusive dealing arrangements without rebates by the same undertakings.

145. See the recent remarks made by Alexander Italianer (then Director General of DG Competition; now Secretary-General of the European Commission since 1 September 2015) at the Charles River Associates Conference on 10 December 2014 (Italianer, *supra* note 91, pp. 11-12).

146. It will be interesting to see the approach to be adopted by the Commission in the most recent formal investigation involving exclusivity rebates, initiated against Qualcomm, in special how it will apply the concepts and standards of the *Guidance* to assess the investigated conduct. In December 2015, the Commission sent a Statement of Objection (SO) to Qualcomm on exclusivity payment (simultaneously with other SO on predatory pricing). According to the Commission, since 2011, Qualcomm has paid significant amounts to a major smartphone and tablet

3.6 Conditionality of the rebate

According to the judgment, a rebate system will be considered 'conditional upon exclusivity' even when there is no written agreement or evidence that the rebates were the decisive factor in the customer's choice of its supplier, or when the rebates were not a unilateral imposition by the dominant undertaking, but were the result of customers' requests.

In terms of the absence of a written agreement, the General Court remembered that, according to *Hoffmann-La Roche*, "an undertaking in a dominant position abuses that position if it applies an exclusivity rebate system even without tying the purchasers by a formal obligation"[147].

Moreover, the Court also stressed that the application of the legal standards for assessment of exclusivity rebates is not prevented by the absence of evidence that the rebates were the sole or decisive reason for the customer's behaviour when using the dominant undertaking as its exclusive supplier. Even where there is evidence that customer's purchasing decision was influenced by other factors (such as quality, reliability etc.), such evidence would at best deny the existence of a causal link between the exclusivity rebate and the customer's behavior, but not the existence of an exclusivity rebate practice, which is sufficient for the application of the legal standards of the settled case-law[148].

Therefore, in order to establish the 'conditional nature' of a rebate system, it is sufficient that the undertaking in a dominant position "indicates in a credible manner to its customer that the grant of a financial advantage depends on exclusive or quasi-exclusive supply"[149].

Accordingly, concerning the relevance of the amount of rebate offered to customers, the Court observed that this does not affect the finding of the

manufacturer on condition that it exclusively use Qualcomm baseband chipsets in its smartphones and tablets. The Commission has taken the preliminary view that this conduct has reduced the manufacturer's incentives to source chipsets from Qualcomm's competitors and has harmed competition and innovation in the markets for UMTS and LTE baseband chipsets (see press release IP/15/6271, 'Antitrust: Commission sends two Statements of Objections on exclusivity payments and predatory pricing to Qualcomm (8 December 2015), available at: europa.eu/rapid/press-release_IP-15-6271_en.htm).

147. *Intel* judgment, para 106.

148. *Ibid.*, para 543.

149. *Ibid.*, para 106.

'conditional nature' of the practice, provided that there is evidence that the rebate is capable of inducing (or constitutes an incentive for) the customer to purchase exclusively from the dominant undertaking[150].

Furthermore, referring again to *Hoffmann-La Roche*, the Court underlined that the fact that customers themselves were powerful companies and that the rebates represented a response to requests and to customers' buying power did not preclude the existence of an abuse, as it is not justification for subjecting the rebates to the obligation of obtaining supplies exclusively from the dominant undertaking[151]. The Court also rebutted the argument that this position would deny customers an important bargaining tool to obtain lower prices, since customers would continue to be free to bargain for rebates based on the volume of their purchases – which benefits from presumption of legality.

3.7 Exclusivity even if only a market segment is covered

A controverted aspect of the *Intel* judgment refers to the percentage of a customer's total demand that is affected by the conduct in order to determine whether there is an exclusivity condition.

In the case of the customer HP, the General Court found that there was an exclusivity condition irrespective of the fact that the conduct affected only a market segment (corporate desktop computers) that represented around 28% of HP's total demand for x86 CPUs[152].

The Court emphasised that requiring a customer to purchase products pertaining to a certain segment of the market exclusively from the dominant supplier is not equivalent to requiring that customer to purchase 28% of its demand in all market segments from the same supplier[153].

Recalling the relevance of the restrictive effects on customers' freedom of choice in the context of the legal assessment of abuses of dominance, the Court highlighted that even if CPUs for different segments were interchangeable, HP would still be prevented by Intel from using AMD's

150. *Ibid.*, paras 108-109.

151. *Ibid.*, para 139.

152. *Ibid.*, paras 126-134.

153. Intel required HP to purchase 95% of its corporate desktop x86 CPU demand. *Ibid.*, para 125.

CPUs for more than 5% of its corporate desktop business. According to the Court, "the fact that HP's freedom of choice was not limited in those [other] segments of the market does not call into question the fact that HP's freedom of choice was limited in the corporate desktop segment"[154].

Critics argue that the Court's position is excessively strict at this point. Indeed, the general terms in which the Court formulated its position imply that any rebate arrangement conditional on exclusivity for any minimal specific part of the customer's demand would be, by itself, sufficient to infringe Article 102, even though it did not constitute a separate relevant market and consisted of only a small segment of the customer's total demand for the relevant product.

Although not explicit in the judgment, General Court's strict position might have been influenced by the finding that the conduct was part of an overall strategy designed to exclude AMD from access to certain market segments and to customers that were considered key, such as HP[155].

154. *Ibid.*, para 131.

155. *Ibid.*, paras 1536-1537, where the Court refuted the argument that the limited market covered would be a contra-indicator of the strategic nature of the conduct: "1536. Second, the applicant relies, on the one hand, on the fact that the infringements covered only a limited share of the market as a contra-indicator of the strategic nature of its conduct. At the hearing, the applicant stated in that regard that, for a part of 2006, the contested decision finds only one illegal practice vis-à-vis MSH and, for the remainder of 2006 and for 2007, the existence of illegal practices only vis-à-vis MSH and Lenovo (see paragraph 1528 [of the judgment]). The applicant added that that decision does not find that Lenovo had strategic importance comparable to Dell's and HP's. Sales of notebooks in the European Union which were potentially affected by its practices vis-à-vis Lenovo were negligible. That is also the case in respect of sales of computers potentially affected by its practices vis-à-vis MSH if those sales are considered in relation to worldwide sales. On the other hand, the applicant relies on the fact that the OEMs concerned increased their purchases from AMD during the period at issue and that that increase was greater than the growth in AMD's sales to the remainder of the market as another contra-indicator of the strategic nature of its conduct. 1537. However, on the one hand, in so far as the applicant claims that the infringements covered only a limited share of the market, it should be noted that a practice may be considered strategic even if it covers only a limited share of the market. In the present case, the strategic nature of the applicant's conduct stems from the fact that it attempted to foreclose AMD from the most important sales channels, namely Dell for the period between December 2002 and December 2005 and HP for the period between November 2002 and May 2005 (see paragraph 182 [of the

If this is not the reason - and the finding of exclusivity for the purposes of Article 102 is not in any way refined by a criterion of minimal significance in relation to the customers' total demand –, then, in fact, the Court will have established a too strict (and undesirable) standard for assessment.

3.8 Market coverage and 'appreciable effect' criterion

Another topic that is subject to severe criticism is the Court's understanding that the percentage of the total market affected by the conduct is irrelevant for the finding of an abuse where exclusivity rebates are concerned.

The General Court stated that there is no *de minimis* threshold under Article 102: that is, even an exclusivity rebate scheme affecting a truly minimal share of demand may constitute an infringement of Article 102 irrespective of any demonstration of an *appreciable* effect resulting from the conduct.

For the Court, "the possible smallness of the parts of the market which are concerned by the practices at issue is not a relevant argument" for the reasons that (i) any further weakening in a market in which the structure of competition has already been weakened by the presence of a dominant operator may constitute an abuse[156], as well as that (ii) customers should have the opportunity to benefit from whatever degree of competition is possible in the market, and competitors should be able to compete on the merits for the entire market and not just for a part of it[157-158].

judgment]). Moreover, with respect to 2006 and 2007, the Court finds that the coherence between the individual infringements of which the overall strategy was composed is not interrupted by the fact that the infringements concerning Lenovo and MSH were less significant than the infringements concerning Dell and HP. That conclusion applies a fortiori given that MSH was particularly strategically important so far as concerned the retail of consumer computers equipped with x86 CPUs in Europe (see paragraphs 183 and 1507 to 1511 [of the judgment]). In any event, it should be recalled that the foreclosed part of the market was on average significant (see paragraphs 187 to 194 [of the judgment])".

156. *Ibid.*, para 116.

157. *Ibid.*, para 117.

158. As stated in the *Intel* judgment, an expert report indicated that Intel's rebates covered, on average, about 14% of total global demand during the infringement

The Court based this conclusion on:

(i) paragraph 123 of *Hoffmann-La Roche*: which merely states that "since the course of conduct under consideration is that of an undertaking occupying a dominant position on a market where for this reason the structure of competition has already been weakened, within the field of application of Article [102] any further weakening of the structure of competition **may** constitute an abuse of a dominant position" (emphasis added); and

(ii) a sentence in the Opinion of Advocate General Mazák in *Tomra* that simply cites the referred paragraph of *Hoffmann-La Roche*, adding that in that judgment the Court would have "rejected the claim to an 'appreciable effect' or *de minimis* threshold under Article 102 TFEU".

Additionally, in the recent *Post Danmark II159,* the Court of Justice stated that "fixing an appreciability (*de minimis*) threshold for the purposes of determining whether there is an abuse of a dominant position is not justified. [...] in order to fall within the scope of [Article 102 TFEU], the anti-competitive effect of a rebate scheme operated by a dominant undertaking must be probable, there being no need to show that it is of a serious or appreciable nature"[160]. According to the decision, the main purpose of a *de minimis* threshold in Article 102 context (i.e. avoiding that prohibition of abuses may apply to conduct the anti-competitive effects of which are only hypothetical or of negligible significance) is satisfied by the fact that "the assessment of whether a rebate scheme is capable of restricting competition must be carried out in the light of all relevant circumstances, [...] which seeks to determine whether the conduct of the

period, which was considered 'significant' by the Court (see para 194). In any event, the Court's conclusion concerning the 'significance' of the market coverage is irrelevant for the legal assessment of the conduct, since it proposes that there is no *de minimis* threshold under Article 102.

159. Case C-23/14 Post Danmark A/S (2015), not yet published ('*Post Danmark II*'). The Court of Justice has been asked to provide a substantive test to establish whether the practice in question – a rebate scheme implemented by the incumbent postal operator in Denmark based on retroactive standardised volume or turnover thresholds – infringes Article 102.

160. *Ibid.*, paras 73 and 74.

dominant undertaking produces an actual or likely exclusionary effect, to the detriment of competition and, thereby, of consumers' interests"[161].

However, such propositions regarding the apparent rejection of the application of an 'appreciable effect' criterion or a *de minimis* threshold under Article 102 look very convincing.

It is difficult to agree that the wording of paragraph 123 of *Hoffmann-La Roche* allows the conclusion that "any further weakening of the structure of the competition" **automatically** constitutes an abuse of a dominant position, even if the conduct is not capable of producing 'appreciable effects' on competition. In reality, paragraph 123 literally suggests that the characterisation of an abuse is a possible consequence ("may constitute an abuse"), not an automatic result in that context. Thus, the application of a *de minimis* threshold under Article 102 would not be incompatible with *Hoffmann-La Roche.*

In addition, it does not appear to contradict the principle of inherent anticompetitive nature of exclusivity rebates and the consequent legal presumption of illegality that requires objective justification to be rebutted. Quite the opposite, a *de minimis* threshold would strengthen the point that the 'form-based' approach to exclusivity practices under Article 102 is essentially different from any 'per se' legality test[162], since it would dilute the proposition that the 'form-based' approach results in prohibition of rebates schemes whose potential harm to effective competition is purely hypothetical or of negligible significance.

Furthermore, all major parts of EU competition law contain thresholds of minimal significance of effects as a pre-requisite of application. According to the EU Merger Regulation, only concentrations that would *significantly* impede effective competition will be declared incompatible with the common market[163]. The prohibition of agreements restricting

161. *Ibid.*, paras 65-69.

162. See Whish, *supra* note 91, p. 2.

163. Article 2 of Council Regulation (EC) No 139/2004 of 20 January 2004 on the control of concentrations between undertakings (the EC Merger Regulation): "1. Concentrations within the scope of this Regulation shall be appraised in accordance with the objectives of this Regulation and the following provisions with a view to establishing whether or not they are compatible with the common market. [...] 2. A concentration which would not significantly impede effective competition in the common market or in a substantial part of it, in particular

competition by object or effect in Article 101(1) TFEU is not applicable when the impact of the agreement on trade between Member States or on competition is not *appreciable*[164]. Article 107(1) TFEU is not applicable to *de minimis* state aid[165].

Therefore, a requirement of minimal significance of effects for the application of Article 102 would be consistent with the fundamental principles and the established rules of EU competition law.

3.9 Duration of the conduct

Intel argued that it would be relevant to consider the short duration of its supply contracts and that some of them could be terminated with 30 days' notice without cause. The General Court rejected both points.

Concerning the alleged short duration of the agreements, the Court noted that, as the exclusivity term was at least one year (extending to more than five years in some cases), it cannot be considered short for the purposes of Article 102[166]. According to the Court, this finding is based on the

as a result of the creation or strengthening of a dominant position, shall be declared compatible with the common market. 3. A concentration which would significantly impede effective competition, in the common market or in a substantial part of it, in particular as a result of the creation or strengthening of a dominant position, shall be declared incompatible with the common market".

164. Commission's Notice on agreements of minor importance which do not appreciably restrict competition under Article 101(1) TFEU (De Minimis Notice), OJ [2014] C 291/1, para 1 ("Article 101(1) of the Treaty on the Functioning of the European Union prohibits agreements between undertakings which may affect trade between Member States and which have as their object or effect the prevention, restriction or distortion of competition within the internal market. The Court of Justice of the European Union has clarified that that provision is not applicable where the impact of the agreement on trade between Member States or on competition is not appreciable"). See *Expedia*, paras 16 ("[i]t is settled case-law that an agreement of undertakings falls outside the prohibition in that provision, however, if it has only an insignificant effect on the market (Case 5/69 Völk v Vervaecke [1969] ECR 295, paragraph 7; Case C-7/95 P John Deere v Commission [1998] ECR I-3111, paragraph 77; Joined Cases C-215/96 and C-216/96 Bagnasco and Others [1999] ECR I-135, paragraph 34; and Case C-238/05 Asnef-Equifax and Administración del Estado [2006] ECR I-11125, paragraph 50)").

165. Commission Regulation (EU) No 1407/2013 of 18 December 2013 on the application of Articles 107 and 108 TFEU to *de minimis* aid.

166. *Intel* judgment, para 113.

principle that any financial incentive for a customer to purchase exclusively from the dominant undertaking constitutes additional interference with the structure of competition in a market and must hence be regarded as abusive[167].

Regarding the possibility of termination with 30 days' notice, the Court considered this irrelevant to the discussion of the effective duration of the conduct, since the right to terminate an agreement does not prevent its actual application until it is exercised[168]. In addition, the relevant criterion for assessment is the total period during whiwch the dominant company adopted exclusivity rebates and payments to customers, and not "the duration of the notice period for terminating a contract or the fixed duration of an individual contract which forms part of a series of successive contracts"[169].

3.10 Objective justification

The General Court made it clear that the use of exclusivity rebates does not constitute an abuse within the meaning of Article 102 if the dominant undertaking can "justify the use of an exclusivity rebate system, in particular by showing that its conduct is objectively necessary or that the potential foreclosure effect that it brings about may be counterbalanced, outweighed even, by advantages in terms of efficiency that also benefit consumers"[170-171].

167. *Ibid.*, para 111.
168. *Ibid.*, para 112.
169. *Ibid.*, para 195.
170. *Ibid.*, para 94.
171. On the conceptual discussion of the possibility that 'abusive conduct' has an 'objective justification', see the Opinion of Advocate General Jacobs in Case C-53/03 *Syfait* [2005] ECR I-4609, para 72: In any event, however, as the Commission submits, it is clear that the Community case-law provides dominant undertakings with the possibility of demonstrating an objective justification for their conduct, even if it is prima facie an abuse, and I now turn to the issue of objective justification. I would add that the two-stage analysis suggested by the distinction between an abuse and its objective justification is to my mind somewhat artificial. Article [102 TFEU], by contrast with Article [101 TFEU], does not contain any explicit provision for the exemption of conduct otherwise falling within it. Indeed, the very fact that conduct is characterised as an 'abuse'

As seen above, the possibility of presenting justifications for the conduct is what distinguishes the 'form-based' approach adopted in the *Intel* judgment from the mere 'per se' illegality[172]. This possibility has always been clear in several judgments by the EU Courts and decisions by the Commission[173]. Thus, the criticism that the General Court has created (or reaffirmed) a 'per se' rule of illegality for exclusivity rebates under Article 102 is inconsistent not only with the terms of the *Intel* judgment, but also with the settled case-law.

In general, there are two types of possible objective justifications under Article 102. A dominant undertaking may claim that its conduct is justified by demonstrating either (i) that it is necessary on the basis of objective factors external to the dominant company, such as for health or safety[174] ('objective necessity defence'), or (ii) that it produces substantial efficiencies also benefiting consumers that counterbalance or even outweigh any potential anticompetitive effects ('efficiency defence').

In both cases, the burden of proof will be on the dominant undertaking[175]. In addition, competition authorities will only admit justifications if the conduct in question is indispensable and proportionate to the goal allegedly pursued by the dominant undertaking[176]. With specific

suggests that a negative conclusion has already been reached, by contrast with the more neutral terminology of 'prevention, restriction, or distortion of competition' under Article [101 TFEU]. In my view, it is therefore more accurate to say that certain types of conduct on the part of a dominant undertaking do not fall within the category of abuse at all. However, given that the Commission has, in the light of some previous Community case-law, developed its submissions in terms of objective justification, it may be convenient for present purposes to assume that structure".

172. See P. Loewenthal, "The Defence of 'Objective Justification' in the Application of Article 82 EC" (2005) 28 World Competition 4, p. 455.

173. See, for example, Case 311/84 *Centre Belge d'Etudes de Marché Telémarketing* v *CLT* [1985] ECR 3261; *BBI/Boosey and Hawkes* OJ [1987] L 286/36; Case C-310/93 P *BPB Industries and British Gypsum* v *Commission* [1995] ECR I-865.

174. The Commission notes that "it is normally the task of public authorities to set and enforce public health and safety standards" (see *Guidance*, para 29).

175. See *Michelin II*, paras 107-109; Case T-201/04 *Microsoft* v *Commission* [2007] ECR II-3601, para 688.

176. *Guidance*, para 28: "In the enforcement of Article [102], the Commission will also examine claims put forward by a dominant undertaking that its conduct is justified (20). A dominant undertaking may do so either by demonstrating

regard to the 'efficiency defence', the *Guidance on Enforcement Priorities* explains that the dominant undertaking is expected to demonstrate, with a sufficient degree of probability and based on verifiable evidence, that the following cumulative conditions are fulfilled:

- the efficiencies have been, or are likely to be, realised as a result of the conduct;
- the conduct is indispensable to the realisation of those efficiencies;
- the efficiencies outweigh any likely negative effects on competition and consumer welfare in the affected markets; and
- the conduct does not eliminate effective competition.

One of the criticisms of the 'form-based' approach to exclusivity rebates under Article 102 is that it would avoid the realisation of efficiencies that would benefit consumers[177]. As seen above, the clear possibility to justify the rebates on the basis of efficiencies shows that such criticism is an exaggeration.

In addition, even if one admits that the 'form-based' approach as adopted in the *Intel* judgment represents an impermeable barrier to efficiency justifications, a real loss of those pro-competitive gains would only occur if and to the extent that the exclusivity rebates are indispensable to the realisation of those gains – that is, only if there are no less anticompetitive alternatives to the conduct (other than the exclusivity rebates) capable of producing the same benefits.

Moreover, most of the efficiencies commonly alleged to result from exclusivity rebates do not necessarily seem to depend on the exclusivity condition[178]. Lower costs deriving from the increase in the quantity supplied to a customer (economies of scale) seem to be equally obtainable by means of (presumed legal) quantity rebates. If the purpose of the rebates

that its conduct is objectively necessary or by demonstrating that its conduct produces substantial efficiencies which outweigh any anti-competitive effects on consumers. In this context, the Commission will assess whether the conduct in question is indispensable and proportionate to the goal allegedly pursued by the dominant undertaking".

177. L. Peeperkorn, "Conditional pricing: Why the General Court is wrong in *Intel* and what the Court of Justice can do to rebalance the assessment of rebates" (2015) 1 Concurrences 43.

178. Wils, *supra* note 90, pp. 24-25.

is to offer lower prices or to improve the quality of products or services offered, in most cases the dominant undertaking would be able to do so without conditioning the rebates to exclusivity.

Notably, Intel did not put forward any evidence of an objective justification for its exclusivity rebates[179].

179. *Intel* judgment, paras 94 and 173.

4
Practical implications of the judgment

The debate on the legal tests and standards applicable to the assessment of exclusivity rebates under Article 102 will continue in the Court of Justice. Several critics hope that Intel's grounds of appeal will persuade the Court to abandon the long-established case-law on exclusivity (or loyalty) rebates to adopt a legality test oriented by the so-called 'effects-based' approach[180]. Meanwhile, undertakings should refer to the *Intel* judgment for the legal parameters applicable to exclusivity rebate practices, not only because of its steady reaffirmation of case-law and neatly legal categorisation of rebate schemes under Article 102, but also because the Commission has immediately started to apply them[181].

In this context, the central element of the legal analysis in the *Intel* judgment (i.e. the anticompetitive nature of exclusivity rebates) and its logical consequence of rejecting the AEC analysis as part of the legality test of such rebates under Article 102 (a novel issue) are not groundbreaking, as they harmonize with settled case-law. However, it is indeed a setback for those expecting a radical shift of the legal approach towards the standards used in the *Guidance*.

Nevertheless, undertakings must also consider that the Commission has also indicated that it will continue to apply the *Guidance* according to the purposes it was intended for: priority settings. In addition, the standards

180. See Geradin, *supra* note 52, p. 1; Rey and Venit, *supra* note 99; P. Ibáñez Colomo, "*Intel* and Article 102 TFEU Case Law: Making Sense of a Perpetual Controversy" (2014) LSE Legal Studies Working Paper No. 29/2014; Petit, *supra* note 53; and Peeperkorn, *supra* note 177.

181. *Supra* note 145.

established there continue to be decisive for the legal assessment of other exclusionary practices such as margin squeeze and selective low pricing[182].

The reasons for declaring the inapplicability of any *de minimis* threshold under Article 102 and for finding exclusivity even when only a specific segment of the market is affected, however, are unconvincing and raise practical concerns, since they imply that even a conduct affecting a truly minimal share of the customer's demand (and maybe limited to a specific market niche) may constitute an infringement of Article 102.

182. See section 3.5 above.

5
Conclusion

Legal analysis of conducts of dominant undertakings is an interesting and challenging endeavour. It is only in the application to a specific case that the vague notion of *abuse of dominance* becomes concrete and meaningful. In *Intel*, the hybrid nature of exclusivity rebates (with both price and non-price elements) poses the intriguing question of which legal test should apply to conducts involving both exclusivity and discounting when adopted by a dominant undertaking.

The *Intel* judgment seems a sensible decision on legal and economic grounds, as it properly identifies exclusivity (and not price) as the source of harm to competition resulting from exclusivity rebates by dominant undertakings. In line with the special responsibility held by dominant undertakings under Article 102 TFEU, if such rebates are not objectively justified, they will constitute an abuse of dominant position, since they cause additional restriction to the residual competition that remains in a market in which the state of competition is already distorted by the very presence of an undertaking that, by definition, has the ability to act independently of its competitors, customers and ultimately of its consumers.

Bibliography

Books

R. Bork, *The Antitrust Paradox: A Policy at War with Itself* (The Free Press, 1993)

N. Economides, 'Tying, Bundling and Loyalty/Requirement Rebates' in *Research Handbook on the Economics of Antitrust Law*, ed. E. Elhauge (Edward Elgar, 2012)

L. Gormsen, *A Principled Approach to Abuse of Dominance in European Competition Law* (Cambridge University Press, 2010)

A. Jones and B. Sufrin, *EU Competition Law: Text, Cases, and Materials* (Oxford University Press, 4th ed, 2010)

G. Monti, *EC Competition Law* (Cambridge University Press, 2007)

R. O'Donoghue and J. Padilla, *The Law and Economics of Article 102 TFEU* (Hart Publishing, 2nd ed, 2013)

V. Rose and D. Bailey (eds), *Bellamy & Child – European Community Law of Competition* (Oxford University Press, 7th ed, 2013)

C. Salomão Filho, *A Legal Theory of Economic Power: Implications for Social and Economic Development* (Eduard Elgar, 2011)

L. von Mises, *Human Action: A Treatise on Economics* (Ludwig Von Mises Institute, 1998)

R. Whish and D. Bailey, *Competition Law* (Oxford University Press, 8th ed, 2015)

H. Zenger, 'Rebates and Competition Law: An Overview of EU and National Law' in *EU Competition Case Law Digest*, ed. F. Jenny (Institute of Competition Law, 2014)

Journal Articles

M. Adam and F. Maier-Rigaud, "The Law and Economics of Article 82 EC and the Commission Guidance Paper on Exclusionary Conduct" (2011) Journal of Competition Law (ZWeR - Zeitschrift für Wettbewerbsrecht), 2009, 1, 131-146.

P. Akman, "Searching for the Long-Lost Soul of Article 82 EC" (2009) 29 Oxford Journal of Legal Studies 2, Vol. 29, Issue 2

O. Andriychuk, "Rediscovering the Spirit of Competition: On the Normative Value of the Competitive Process" (2011) 6 European Competition Journal 3

J. Baker, "Economics and Politics: Perspectives on the Goals and Future of Antitrust" (2013) 81 Fordham Law Review 5

P. Behrens, "The 'Consumer Choice' Paradigm in German Ordoliberalism and its Impact upon EU Competition Law" (2014) Europa-Kolleg Hamburg, Discussion Paper No. 1/14

P. Behrens, "The Ordoliberal Concept of 'Abuse' of a Dominant Position and its Impact on Article 102 TFEU" (2015) Nihoul/Takahashi, Abuse Regulation in Competition Law, Proceedings of the 10th ASCOLA Conference Tokyo 2015, Forthcoming, available at ssrn.com/abstract=2658045

V. Daskalova, "Consumer Welfare in EU Competition Law: What is It (Not) About?" (2015) 11 The Competition Law Review 1

N. Economides, "Tying, Bundling, and Loyalty/Requirement Rebates" (2011) NET Institute Working Paper No. 10-26; NYU Law and Economics Research Paper No. 11-02

N. Economides, "Loyalty/Requirement Rebates and the Antitrust Modernization Commission: What is the Appropriate Liability Standard?" (2009) NET Institute Working Paper No. 09-02; NYU Law and Economics Research Paper No. 09-15

E. Elhauge, "How Loyalty Discounts Can Perversely Discourage Discounting" (2009) 5 Journal of Competition Law & Economics 1

E. Elhauge, "Tying, Bundled Discounts, and the Death of the Single Monopoly Profit Theory" (2009) 123 Harvard Law Review 2

E. Elhauge and A. Wickelgren, "Anticompetitive Market Division through Loyalty Discounts without Buyer Commitment" (2012) Harvard Discussion Paper No. 723

E. Elhauge and A. Wickelgren, "Robust Exclusion through Loyalty Discounts with Buyer Commitment" (2012) Harvard Discussion Paper No. 722

G. Federico, "The Antitrust Treatment of Loyalty Discounts in Europe: Towards a more Economic Approach" (2011) 2 JECLAP 3

S. Gates, "Antitrust by Analogy: Developing Rules for Loyalty Rebates and Bundled Discounts" (2013) 79 Antitrust Law Journal 1

D. Geradin, "Loyalty Rebates after *Intel*: Time for the European Court of Justice to Overrule *Hoffman-La Roche*" (2015) Forthcoming in 11 Journal of Competition Law & Economics; George Mason Law & Economics Research Paper No. 15-15

D. Geradin and C. Pereira Neto, "For a Rigorous 'Effects-Based' Analysis of Vertical Restraints Adopted by Dominant Firms: An Analysis of the EU and Brazilian Competition Law" (2012) available at ssrn.com/abstract=2173735

D. Geradin, "The Decision of the Commission of 13 May 2009 in the *Intel* Case: Where is the Foreclosure and Consumer Harm?" (2009) Tilburg Law and Economic Center (TILEC) Discussion Paper No. 2010-022

D. Geradin, "A Proposed Test for Separating Pro-Competitive Conditional Rebates from Anti-Competitive Ones" (2008) available at ssrn.com/abstract=1315292

L. Gormsen, "Are Anti-competitive Effects Necessary for an Analysis under Article 102 TFEU?" (2013) 36 World Competition 2

L. Gormsen, "The Conflict between Economic Freedom and Consumer Welfare in the Modernisation of Article 82 EC" (2007) 3 European Competition Journal 2

F. Hayek, "Competition as a Discovery Procedure" (2002) 5 The Quarterly Journal of Austrian Economics 3

H. Hovenkamp, "Implementing Antitrust's Welfare Goals" (2013) 81 Fordham Law Review 5

P. Ibáñez Colomo, "*Intel* and Article 102 TFEU Case Law: Making Sense of a Perpetual Controversy" (2014) LSE Legal Studies Working Paper No. 29/2014

P. Ibáñez Colomo, "Post Danmark II, or the Quest for Administrability and Coherence in Article 102 TFEU" (2015), LSE Legal Studies Working Paper No. 15/2015, available at ssrn.com/abstract=2636407

A. Jones, "Left Behind by Modernisation? Restrictions by Object under Article 101(1)" (2011) 649 European Competition Journal 2010

R. Lande, "A Traditional and Textualist Analysis of the Goals of Antitrust: Efficiency, Preventing Theft from Consumers, and Consumer Choice" (2013) 81 Fordham Law Review 5

P. Loewenthal, "The Defence of 'Objective Justification' in the Application of Article 82 EC" (2005) 28 World Competition 4

F. Maier-Rigaud, and U. Schwalbe, "Do Retroactive Rebates Imply Lower Prices for Consumers?" (2013) available at ssrn.com/abstract=2276396

E. Mestmäcker, "A Legal Theory without Law - Posner v. Hayek on Economic Analysis of Law" (2008) available at ssrn.com/abstract=1168422

P. Nihoul, "The Ruling of the General Court in *Intel*: Towards the End of an Effect-based Approach in European Competition Law?" (2014) JECLAP first published online September 15, 2014

P. Nihoul, "Freedom of Choice - The Emergence of a Powerful Concept in European Competition Law" (2012) available at ssrn.com/abstract=2077694

B. Orbach, "The Antitrust Consumer Welfare Paradox" (2011) 7 Journal of Competition Law & Economics 1

L. Peeperkorn, "Conditional pricing: Why the General Court is wrong in *Intel* and what the Court of Justice can do to rebalance the assessment of rebates" (2015) 1 Concurrences 43

N. Petit, "*Intel*, Leveraging Rebates and the Goals of Article 102 TFEU" (2015) available at ssrn.com/abstract=2567628

P. Rey and J. Venit, "An Effects-Based Approach to Article 102: A Response to Wouter Wils" (2015) 38 World Competition 1

A. Sen, "Markets and Freedoms: Achievements and Limitations of the Market Mechanism in Promoting Individual Freedoms" (1993) 45 Oxford Economic Papers 4

J. Venit, "Case T-286/09 *Intel* v *Commission* – The Judgment of the General Court: All Steps Backward and No Steps Forward" (2014) 10 European Competition Journal 2

J. Weiler, 'The Transformation of Europe" (1991) 100 The Yale Law Journal 8

O. Williamson, "Allocative Efficiency and the Limits of Antitrust" (1969) 59 The American Economic Review 2

W. Wils, "Discretion and Prioritisation in Public Antitrust Enforcement, in Particular EU Antitrust Enforcement" (2011) 34 World Competition: Law and Economics Review 3

W. Wils, "The Judgment of the EU General Court in *Intel* and the So-Called 'More Economic Approach' to Abuse of Dominance" (2014) 37 World Competition: Law and Economics Review 4

R. Whish, "*Intel* v *Commission*: Keep Calm and Carry on!" (2015) 6 JECLAP 1

R. Whish, "Regulation 2790/99: The Commission's 'New Style' Block Exemption for Vertical Agreements" (2000) 37 CMLR 887

J. Wright and D. Ginsburg, "The Goals of Antitrust: Welfare Trumps Choice" (2013) 81 Fordham Law Review 5

H. Zenger, "Loyalty Rebates and the Competitive Process" (2012) 8 Journal of Competition Law & Economics 4

Cases

Judgments of the Court of Justice

Joined Cases 56/64 and 58/64 *Consten and Grundig* v *Commission* [1966] ECR 299

Case 5/69 *Völk* v *Vervaecke* [1969] ECR 295

Case 22/71 *Béguelin Import Co* v *GL Import-Export SA* [1971] ECR 949

Case 85/76 *Hoffmann-La Roche* v *Commission* [1979] ECR 461

Case 322/81 *Nederlandsche Banden Industrie Michelin* v *Commission* [1983] ECR 3461

Case 311/84 *Centre Belge d'Etudes de Marché Telémarketing* v *CLT* [1985] ECR 3261

Case 27/76 *United Brands* v *Commission* [1987] ECR 207

Case C-234/89 *Delimitis* v *Henninger Brau* [1991] ECR I-935

Case C-62/86 *AKZO Chemie BV* v *Commission* [1991] ECR I-3359

Case C-310/93 P *BPB Industries and British Gypsum* v *Commission* [1995] ECR I-865

Case C-95/04 P *British Airways* v *Commission* [2007] ECR I-2331

Case C-209/07 *Beef Industry Development Society and Barry Brothers* [2008] ECR I-8637

Case C-202/07 P *France Télécom* v *Commission* [2009] ECR I-2369

Case C-8/08 *T-Mobile Netherlands and Others* [2009] ECR I-4529

Case C-280/08 P *Deutsche Telekom* v *Commission* [2010] ECR I-9555

Case C-52/09 *TeliaSonera Sverige* [2011] ECR I-527

Case C-496/09 *Commission* v *Italy* [2011] ECR I-11483

Case C-549/10 P *Tomra Systems and Others* v *Commission* [2012] ECR

Case C-209/10 *Post Danmark* [2012] ECR

Case C-226/11 *Expedia* v *Autorité de la concurrence* [2012] ECR

Case C-23/14 *Post Danmark A/S* [2015], not yet published

Judgments of the General Court of the European Union

Case T-65/89 *BPB Industries and British Gypsum* v *Commission* [1993] ECR II-389

Case T-203/01 *Michelin* v *Commission* [2003] ECR II-04071

Case T-219/99 *British Airways* v *Commission* [2003] ECR II-5917

Case T-201/04 *Microsoft* v *Commission* [2007] ECR II-3601

Case T-155/06 *Tomra Systems and Others* v *Commission* [2010] ECR II-4361

Case T-286/09 *Intel Corp.* v *Commission* [2014], not yet published

Opinions of Advocate General

Opinion of Advocate General Jacobs in Case C-53/03 *Syfait*, delivered on 28 October 2004

Opinion of Advocate General Mazák in Case C-549/10 P *Tomra Systems and Others* v *Commission*, delivered on 2 February 2012

Opinion of Advocate General Kokott in Case C-23/14 *Post Danmark A/S*, delivered on 21 May 2015

Decisions of the European Commission

Case COMP/C-3/37.990 – *Intel*, Decision of 13 May 2009, OJ [2009] C 227

Other sources

European Commission, communication from the Commission: "Guidance on the Commission's enforcement priorities in applying Article [102 TFEU] to abusive exclusionary conduct by dominant undertakings", OJ [2009] C 45/7

European Commission, communication from the Commission: "Notice on agreements of minor importance which do not appreciably restrict competition under Article 101(1) of the Treaty on the Functioning of the European Union – 'De Minimis Notice'", OJ [2014] C 291/01

Economic Advisory Group on Competition Policy (EAGCP), report: "An economic approach to Article 82" (2005) available at ec.europa.eu/dgs/competition/economist/eagcp_july_21_05.pdf

ICN, *Unilateral Conduct Workbook - Chapter 1: The Objectives and Principles of Unilateral Conduct Laws* (2012), available at www.internationalcompetitionnetwork.org/uploads/library/doc827.pdf

ICN, "Report on the Analysis of Loyalty Discounts and Rebates Under Unilateral Conduct Laws" (2009) presented at the 8th Annual Conference of the ICN, Zurich, available at internationalcompetitionnetwork.org/uploads/library/doc357.pdf

A. Italianer, "The Object of Effects" (2014) Speech at Charles River Associates Conference, Brussels, 10 December 2014, available at ec.europa.eu/competition/speeches/text/sp2014_07_en.pdf

N. Kroes, "Preliminary Thoughts on Policy Review of Article 82" (2005) Speech at the Fordham Corporate Law Institute, New York, 23 September 2005, available at www.europa.eu/rapid/press-release_SPEECH-05-537_en.htm.

OECD, report: "Policy Roundtables Report on Fidelity and Bundled Rebates and Discount" (2008) available at oecd.org/competition/abuse/41772877.pdf

J. Wright, "Simple but Wrong or Complex but More Accurate? The Case for an Exclusive Dealing-Based Approach to Evaluating Loyalty Discounts" (2013) Speech at Bates White 10th Annual Antitrust Conference, Washington, DC, 3 June 2013, available ftc.gov/sites/default/files/documents/public_statements/simple-wrong-or-complex-more-accurate-case-exclusive-dealing-based-approach-evaluating-loyalty/130603bateswhite.pdf

Extract of the *Intel* judgment

Contents

JUDGMENT OF THE GENERAL COURT
(Seventh Chamber, Extended Composition)

12 June 2014

(Competition — Abuse of dominant position — Microprocessors market — Decision finding an infringement of Article 82 EC and Article 54 of the EEA Agreement — Loyalty rebates — 'Naked' restrictions — Classification as abuse — As-efficient-competitor analysis — Commission's international jurisdiction — Obligation on the Commission to investigate — Limits — Rights of the defence — Principle of sound administration — Overall strategy — Fines — Single and continuous infringement — 2006 Guidelines on the method of setting fines)

In Case T-286/09,

Intel Corp., established in Wilmington, Delaware (United States), represented initially by K. Bacon, Barrister, M. Hoskins, N. Green QC, S. Singla, Barrister, I. Forrester QC, A. Parr, R. Mackenzie, Solicitors, and D. Piccinin, Barrister, and subsequently by I. Forrester, A. Parr, R. Mackenzie and D. Piccinin,

applicant,

supported by

Association for Competitive Technology, Inc., established in Washington, DC (United States), represented by J.-F. Bellis, lawyer,

intervener,

v

European Commission, represented by T. Christoforou, V. Di Bucci, N. Khan and M. Kellerbauer, acting as Agents,

defendant,

supported by

Union fédérale des consommateurs — Que choisir (UFC — Que choisir), established in Paris (France), represented initially by J. Franck, and subsequently by E. Nasry, lawyers, intervener,

ACTION for annulment of Commission Decision C(2009) 3726 final of 13 May 2009 relating to a proceeding under Article 82 [EC] and Article 54 of the EEA Agreement (Case COMP/C-3/37.990 — *Intel*) or, alternatively, annulment or reduction of the fine imposed on the applicant,

THE GENERAL COURT (Seventh Chamber, Extended Composition),

composed of A. Dittrich (Rapporteur), President, I. Wiszniewska-Białecka, M. Prek, J. Schwarcz and M. Kancheva, Judges,

Registrar: E. Coulon and J. Weychert, Administrator,

having regard to the written procedure and further to the hearing on 3 to 6 July 2012, gives the following

Judgment

Background to the dispute

1 The applicant, Intel Corp., is a US-based company that designs, develops, manufactures, and markets central processing units ('CPUs'), 'chipsets', and other semiconductor components, as well as platform solutions for data processing and communications devices.

2 At the end of 2008, Intel employed about 94 100 people worldwide. In 2007, Intel had net revenues of USD 38 334 million and a net income of USD 6 976 million. In 2008, Intel had net revenues of USD 37 586 million and a net income of USD 5 292 million.

I – Administrative procedure

3 On 18 October 2000, Advanced Micro Devices ('AMD') submitted a formal complaint to the Commission of the European Communities under Article 3 of Council Regulation (EEC) No 17 of 6 February 1962, First Regulation implementing Articles [81 EC] and [82 EC] (OJ, English Special Edition, 1959–1962(I), p. 87), which it further supplemented by putting forward new facts and allegations, in the context of a supplementary complaint of 26 November 2003.

4 In May 2004, the Commission launched a round of investigations relating to elements in AMD's supplementary complaint. Within the framework of that investigation, in July 2005, the Commission, assisted by several national competition authorities, carried out on-the-spot inspections under Article 20(4) of Council Regulation (EC) No 1/2003 of

16 December 2002 on the implementation of the rules on competition laid down in Articles 81 [EC] and 82 [EC] (OJ 2003 L 1, p. 1) at four Intel locations, in the United Kingdom, Germany, Italy and Spain, as well as at the locations of several Intel customers, in France, Germany, Italy, Spain and the United Kingdom.

5 On 17 July 2006, AMD filed a complaint with the Bundeskartellamt (German Federal Cartel Office), in which it claimed that Intel had engaged inter alia in exclusionary marketing arrangements with Media-Saturn-Holding GmbH ('MSH'), a European retailer of microelectronic devices and the largest desktop computer distributor in Europe. The Bundeskartellamt exchanged information with the Commission on this subject, pursuant to Article 12 of Regulation No 1/2003.

6 On 23 August 2006, the Commission held a meeting with Mr D1 [confidential] (2) of Dell Inc., a customer of Intel. The Commission did not place the indicative list of topics for the meeting ('the indicative list of topics') on the case file and did not take minutes of it. A member of the team responsible for the file at the Commission drafted a note which was described as internal by the Commission ('the internal note') concerning that meeting. On 19 December 2008, the Commission provided the applicant with a non-confidential version of that note.

7 On 26 July 2007, the Commission notified to the applicant a statement of objections ('the Statement of Objections of 2007') concerning its conduct vis-à-vis five major original equipment manufacturers ('OEMs'), namely Dell, Hewlett-Packard Company (HP), Acer Inc., NEC Corp. and International Business Machines Corp. (IBM). Intel replied to that statement of objections on 7 January 2008, and an oral hearing was held on 11 and 12 March 2008. Access to the file was granted three times to Intel, namely on 31 July 2007, 23 July 2008 and 19 December 2008.

8 The Commission undertook several investigative measures relating to AMD's allegations, including on-the-spot inspections at the sites of several computer retailers and of Intel in February 2008. In addition, several written requests for information were addressed, pursuant to Article 18 of Regulation No 1/2003, to a number of major OEMs.

9 On 17 July 2008, the Commission issued to the applicant a supplementary statement of objections concerning its conduct vis-à-vis MSH. That statement of objections ('the Supplementary Statement of Objections of

2008') also covered Intel's conduct vis-à-vis Lenovo Group Ltd ('Lenovo') and included new evidence on Intel's conduct vis-à-vis some of the OEMs covered by the Statement of Objections of 2007, which had been obtained by the Commission after the publication of the latter.

10 The Commission originally set Intel a deadline of eight weeks to submit its reply to the Supplementary Statement of Objections of 2008. On 15 September 2008, that deadline was extended to 17 October 2008 by the Hearing Officer.

11 Intel did not reply to the Supplementary Statement of Objections of 2008 within the prescribed period. However, on 10 October 2008, Intel lodged an application with the General Court, registered under reference T-457/08, requesting the Court, first, to annul two decisions of the Commission relating to the setting of the period for replying to the Supplementary Statement of Objections of 2008 and to the Commission's refusal to obtain several categories of documents emanating inter alia from the file of the private litigation between Intel and AMD in the US State of Delaware and, second, to extend the deadline for lodging its reply to the Supplementary Statement of Objections of 2008 in order to have a period of 30 days from the day on which it obtained access to the relevant documents.

12 Intel further lodged an application for interim measures, registered under reference T-457/08 R, by which it sought to obtain the suspension of the Commission's procedure pending the judgment on its substantive application, as well as the suspension of the period set for lodging its reply to the Supplementary Statement of Objections of 2008 and, in the alternative, that it be allowed a period of 30 days from the date of that judgment in order to reply to the Supplementary Statement of Objections of 2008.

13 On 19 December 2008, the Commission sent Intel a letter drawing its attention to a number of specific items of evidence which the Commission intended to use in a potential final Decision ('the Letter of Facts'). Intel did not reply to that letter by the deadline of 23 January 2009.

14 On 27 January 2009, the President of the Court dismissed the application for interim measures (order of the President of the Court of 27 January 2009 in Case T-457/08 R Intel v Commission, not published in the ECR). Following that order, on 29 January 2009, Intel proposed to file its reply to the Supplementary Statement of Objections of 2008 and to the Letter of Facts within 30 days of the order of the President of the Court.

15 On 2 February 2009, the Commission informed Intel by letter that the Commission services had decided not to grant an extension of the deadlines to reply to the Supplementary Statement of Objections of 2008 or to the Letter of Facts. The letter of 2 February 2009 also stated that the Commission services were nevertheless willing to consider the possible relevance of belated written submissions, provided that Intel served such submissions by 5 February 2009. Finally, the Commission took the view that it was not obliged to grant a request for a hearing lodged out of time and that its services considered that the proper conduct of the administrative procedure did not necessitate an oral hearing.

16 On 3 February 2009, Intel withdrew its action in the main proceedings in Case T-457/08 and the case was removed from the register by order of the President of the Fifth Chamber of the Court of 24 March 2009.

17 On 5 February 2009, Intel served a written submission including observations relating to the Supplementary Statement of Objections of 2008 and the Letter of Facts, which it classed as a 'reply to the Supplementary Statement of Objections [of 2008]' and a 'reply to the [Letter of Facts]'.

18 On 10 February 2009, Intel wrote to the Hearing Officer and asked to be granted an oral hearing in relation to the Supplementary Statement of Objections of 2008. The Hearing Officer rejected the request by letter of 17 February 2009.

19 On 13 May 2009, the Commission adopted Decision C(2009) 3726 final relating to a proceeding under Article 82 [EC] and Article 54 of the EEA Agreement (Case COMP/C-3/37.990 — Intel) ('the contested decision'), a summary of which appears in the Official Journal of the European Union (OJ 2009 C 227, p. 13).

II – Contested decision

20 According to the contested decision, Intel committed a single and continuous infringement of Article 82 EC and Article 54 of the Agreement on the European Economic Area (EEA), from October 2002 until December 2007, by implementing a strategy aimed at foreclosing a competitor, AMD, from the market for x86 CPU microprocessors ('x86 CPUs').

A – Relevant market

21 The products concerned by the contested decision are CPUs. The CPU is a key component of any computer, both in terms of overall performance

and cost of the system. It is often referred to as a computer's 'brain'. The manufacturing process of CPUs requires expensive high-tech facilities.

22 CPUs used in computers can be sub-divided into two categories, namely x86 CPUs and CPUs based on another architecture. x86 architecture is a standard designed by Intel for its CPUs. It can run both the Windows and Linux operating systems. Windows is primarily linked to the x86 instruction set. Prior to 2000, there were several manufacturers of x86 CPUs. However, most of these manufacturers have since exited the market. The contested decision states that, since then, Intel and AMD have been essentially the only two companies still manufacturing x86 CPUs.

23 The Commission's inquiry led to the conclusion that the relevant product market was not wider than the market of x86 CPUs. The contested decision leaves open the question whether there is a single x86 CPU market for all computers or whether it is necessary to draw a distinction between three separate x86 CPU markets, namely the market for desktop computers, the market for notebook computers and the market for servers. According to the contested decision, given Intel's market shares for each segment, there is no difference to the conclusion on dominance.

24 The geographical market has been defined as worldwide.

B – Dominant position

25 In the contested decision, the Commission finds that, in the 10-year period which was examined (1997-2007), Intel consistently held market shares in excess of or around 70%. Furthermore, according to the contested decision, there are significant barriers to entry and expansion in the x86 CPU market. They arise from sunk investments in research and development, intellectual property and the production facilities that are necessary to produce x86 CPUs. In consequence, all Intel's competitors, except AMD, have exited the market or are left with an insignificant share.

26 On the basis of Intel's market shares and the barriers to entry and expansion in the relevant market, the contested decision concludes that at least in the period covered by that decision, that is to say from October 2002 to December 2007, Intel held a dominant position in that market.

C – Abuse and fine

27 The contested decision describes two types of Intel conduct vis-à-vis its trading partners, namely conditional rebates and 'naked restrictions'.

28 First, according to the contested decision, Intel awarded four OEMs, namely Dell, Lenovo, HP and NEC, rebates which were conditioned on these OEMs purchasing all or almost all of their x86 CPUs from Intel. Similarly, Intel awarded payments to MSH, which were conditioned on MSH selling exclusively computers containing Intel's x86 CPUs.

29 The contested decision concludes that the conditional rebates granted by Intel constitute fidelity rebates. With regard to Intel's conditional payments to MSH, the contested decision establishes that the economic mechanism of these payments is equivalent to that of the conditional rebates to OEMs.

30 The contested decision also conducts an economic analysis of the capability of the rebates to foreclose a hypothetical competitor as efficient as Intel (as-efficient-competitor test; 'the AEC test'), albeit not dominant. More precisely, the test establishes at what price a competitor as efficient as Intel would have had to offer CPUs in order to compensate an OEM for the loss of an Intel rebate. The same kind of analysis was conducted for the Intel payments to MSH.

31 The evidence gathered by the Commission led it to the conclusion that Intel's conditional rebates and payments induced the loyalty of the key OEMs and of MSH. The effects of these practices were complementary, in that they significantly diminished competitors' ability to compete on the merits of their x86 CPUs. Intel's anti-competitive conduct thereby resulted in a reduction of consumer choice and in lower incentives to innovate.

32 Second, with regard to naked restrictions, the Commission states that Intel awarded three OEMs, namely HP, Acer and Lenovo, payments which were conditioned on these OEMs postponing or cancelling the launch of AMD CPU-based products and/or putting restrictions on the distribution of those products. The contested decision concludes that Intel's conduct also directly harmed competition, and did not constitute normal competition on the merits.

33 The Commission concludes in the contested decision that, in each instance, Intel's conduct vis-à-vis the OEMs mentioned above and MSH constitutes an abuse under Article 82 EC, but that each of those individual abuses are also part of a single strategy aimed at foreclosing AMD, Intel's only significant competitor, from the market for x86 CPUs. Those individual abuses are therefore part of a single infringement of Article 82 EC.

34 By applying the Guidelines on the method of setting fines imposed pursuant to Article 23(2)(a) of Regulation No 1/2003 (OJ 2006 C 210, p. 2; 'the 2006 Guidelines'), the Commission imposed on the applicant a fine of EUR 1.06 billion (as regards the calculation of the fine, see paragraphs 1554 to 1558 below).

D – Operative part

35 The operative part of the contested decision reads as follows:

'Article 1

Intel … has committed a single and continuous infringement of Article 82 [EC] and Article 54 of the EEA Agreement from October 2002 until December 2007 by implementing a strategy aimed at foreclosing competitors from the market of x86 CPUs which consisted of the following elements:

(a) Granting rebates to Dell between December 2002 and December 2005 at a level that was conditional on Dell obtaining all of its x86 CPU supplies from Intel;

(b) Granting rebates to HP between November 2002 and May 2005 at a level that was conditional on HP obtaining at least 95% of its corporate desktop x86 CPU supplies from Intel;

(c) Granting rebates to NEC between October 2002 and November 2005 at a level that was conditional on NEC obtaining at least 80% of its client PC x86 CPU supplies from Intel;

(d) Granting rebates to Lenovo between January 2007 and December 2007 at a level that was conditional on Lenovo obtaining all of its notebook x86 CPU supplies from Intel;

(e) Granting payments to [MSH] between October 2002 and December 2007 at a level that was conditional on [MSH] selling only computers incorporating Intel x86 CPUs;

(f) Granting payments to HP between November 2002 and May 2005 conditional on: (i) HP directing HP's AMD-based x86 CPU business desktops to Small and Medium Business and Government, and Educational and Medical customers rather than to enterprise business customers; (ii) precluding HP's channel partners from stocking HP's AMD-based x86 CPU business desktops such that such desktops would only be available to customers by ordering them from HP (either directly or via HP channel partners acting as sales agent); and (iii) HP delaying the launch of its AMD-based x86 CPU business desktop in the [Europe, Middle East and Africa] region by six months;

(g) Granting payments to Acer between September 2003 and January 2004 conditional on Acer delaying an AMD-based x86 CPU notebook;

(h) Granting payments to Lenovo between June 2006 and December 2006 conditional on Lenovo delaying and finally cancelling its AMD-based x86 CPU notebooks.

Article 2

For the infringement referred to in Article 1, a fine of EUR 1 060 000 000 is imposed on Intel …

Article 3

Intel … shall immediately bring to an end the infringement referred to in Article 1 in so far as it has not already done so.

Intel … shall refrain from repeating any act or conduct described in Article 1, and from any act or conduct having the same or equivalent object or effect.

…'

Procedure and forms of order sought

36 By application lodged at the Court Registry on 22 July 2009, the applicant brought the present action.

37 By document lodged at the Court Registry on 14 October 2009, AMD sought leave to intervene in the present proceedings in support of the Commission. However, on 16 November 2009, AMD informed the Court that it was withdrawing its application to intervene in the case. In consequence, by order of the President of the Eighth Chamber of the Court of 5 January 2010, AMD was removed from the case as intervener.

38 By document lodged at the Court Registry on 30 October 2009, the Union fédérale des consommateurs — Que choisir (UFC — Que choisir) ('UFC') sought leave to intervene in the present proceedings in support of the Commission. By order of 7 June 2010, the President of the Eighth Chamber of the Court granted leave. By letter lodged at the Court Registry on 22 September 2010, UFC informed the Court that it would not be lodging

a statement in intervention but that it would make oral submissions at the hearing.

39 By document lodged at the Court Registry on 2 November 2009, the Association for Competitive Technology ('ACT') sought leave to intervene in the present proceedings in support of Intel. By order of 7 June 2010, the President of the Eighth Chamber of the Court granted leave. ACT submitted its statement in intervention within the prescribed period and the main parties submitted their observations on that statement.

40 Following a change in the composition of the Chambers of the Court, the Judge-Rapporteur was assigned to the Seventh Chamber, to which the present case was accordingly allocated.

41 By decision of 18 January 2012, the Court referred the case to the Seventh Chamber sitting in extended composition, pursuant to Article 14(1) and Article 51(1) of its Rules of Procedure.

42 Upon hearing the Report of the Judge-Rapporteur, the Court decided to open the oral procedure and, by way of measures of organisation of procedure provided for in Article 64 of the Rules of Procedure, put written questions to the parties and requested the applicant and the Commission to produce certain documents. The applicant, the Commission and ACT replied to the written questions and produced the documents requested within the period prescribed.

43 UFC's reply to a written question put by the Court having been lodged at the Court Registry outside the prescribed period, by decision of 1 June 2012, the President of the Seventh Chamber decided that that reply would nevertheless be placed on the file.

44 By order of 16 April 2012, the Court ordered the Commission, pursuant to Article 65(b), Article 66(1) and the second subparagraph of Article 67(3) of the Rules of Procedure, to produce the confidential version of the internal note concerning the meeting between Commission agents and Mr D1, [confidential] of Dell of 23 August 2006. The Commission complied within the prescribed period. That document was not initially communicated to the applicant or the interveners.

45 Intel and the Commission requested that certain confidential matters contained in their pleadings and annexes, including replies to the written questions of the Court, not be communicated to the interveners. Only the non-confidential versions of those pleadings and annexes produced by the

applicant and the Commission were communicated to the interveners. The interveners raised no objections in that regard.

46 On 7 June 2012, the applicant, the Commission and ACT attended, in the presence of the five Members of the Seventh Chamber sitting in extended composition, an informal meeting concerning the confidential treatment of certain information and the organisation of the hearing.

47 By letter registered at the Court Registry on 2 July 2012, the applicant stated that the various OEMs concerned as well as MSH and AMD agreed to information concerning them previously identified as confidential being disclosed during the part of the hearing which would be conducted in public and in the public version of the future judgment, subject to certain exceptions.

48 The parties presented oral argument and their answers to the questions put by the Court at the hearing which took place, partly in camera, from 3 to 6 July 2012.

49 By order of 29 January 2013, the oral procedure was reopened. By way of measures of organisation of procedure, the Commission, which had in turn consulted Dell, having been heard and not having raised any objections, the Court notified to the applicant and the interveners the full version of the internal note concerning the meeting with Mr D1, [confidential] of Dell, and requested that they submit their observations on the parts of that note which had not been sent to them previously. The applicant and ACT complied with that request within the prescribed period. UFC did not submit observations within the prescribed period. The Court then requested the Commission to submit its comments on the applicant's observations. The Commission complied with that request within the prescribed period. The Court also requested the applicant and the Commission to submit their comments on ACT's observations. The applicant and the Commission did so within the prescribed period. The oral procedure was then closed on 6 May 2013.

50 The applicant, supported by ACT, claims that the Court should:

- annul the contested decision in whole or in part;
- in the alternative, annul or substantially reduce the amount of the fine imposed;
- order the Commission to pay the costs.

51 The Commission contends that the Court should:

- dismiss the action;
- order the applicant to pay the costs;
- order ACT to pay the costs relating to its intervention.

52 UFC concurs in essence with the form of order sought by the Commission and contends that the applicant should be ordered to pay the costs.

Law

I – Admissibility of certain annexes

53 The Commission claims that certain documents submitted by the applicant as annexes to the application, which consist of testimonies made before the Delaware court before which the United States proceedings were brought ('the Delaware court', see paragraph 11 above), are inadmissible under Article 43(5) of the Rules of Procedure, according to which '[w]here in view of the length of a document only extracts from it are annexed to the pleading, the whole document or a full copy of it shall be lodged at the Registry'.

54 The Commission states that the applicant has not provided or lodged at the Registry the annexes to the depositions made before the Delaware court. The Commission states moreover that, in respect of some of those testimonies, the applicant provided only extracts from the transcript instead of the full transcript.

55 It is necessary to reject at the outset the Commission's line of argument in so far as it concerns the testimonies the transcript of which was submitted in its entirety, but without their annexes. According to Article 43(5) of the Rules of Procedure, it is sufficient to lodge the full document at the Registry. That article does not require that all the other documents to which a document annexed to a pleading refers also be lodged at the Registry. In cases where certain parts of the testimonies on which the applicant relies are not comprehensible without access to the documents to which the witnesses refer, that would concern only the probative value of the parts of the testimonies concerned. However, that cannot call in question the admissibility of the testimonies produced by the applicant in annex to its application.

56 As regards the testimonies in respect of which the applicant only produced extracts annexed to its pleadings, the Court makes the following observations.

57 Even if Article 43(5) of the Rules of Procedure were to be interpreted as imposing an obligation on the parties to lodge a full version at the Registry of any document of which they submit extracts annexed to a pleading, any infringement of that obligation could in any event be rectified.

58 In that regard, it should be observed that, according to point 57(d) of the Practice directions to parties adopted by the General Court on 5 July 2007 (OJ 2007 L 232, p. 7), as amended, even a failure to produce annexes mentioned in the schedule is capable of being rectified. The production of only an extract of a document by a party instead of the full document constitutes a fortiori a defect which is capable of being rectified.

59 In the present case, the Court requested the applicant, by way of a measure of organisation of procedure, to produce the full versions of all the testimonies of which the applicant had submitted only extracts and of which it had not lodged a full version at the Registry. The applicant complied with that request within the prescribed period and the Court gave the Commission an opportunity to submit its observations on those documents in writing.

60 The Commission's argument that some of the documents produced by the applicant are inadmissible under Article 43(5) of the Rules of Procedure must therefore be rejected.

II – The heads of claim for annulment of the contested decision

A – Horizontal questions concerning the legal assessments carried out by the Commission

1. The burden of proof and the standard of proof required

61 The applicant refers to the case-law of the European Union Courts and states, inter alia, that competition cases of the same nature as the present case are of a penal nature, which means that a high standard of proof and the presumption of innocence apply.

62 According to Article 2 of Regulation No 1/2003, in any proceedings for the application of Article 82 EC, the burden of proving an infringement of that article rests on the party or the authority alleging the infringement,

namely, in the present case, the Commission. Furthermore, according to well settled case-law, any doubt in the mind of the Court must operate to the advantage of the undertaking to which the decision finding an infringement was addressed. The Court cannot therefore conclude that the Commission has established the infringement at issue to the requisite legal standard if it still entertains any doubts on that point, in particular in proceedings for annulment of a decision imposing a fine (Joined Cases T-67/00, T-68/00, T-71/00 and T-78/00 JFE Engineering and Others v Commission [2004] ECR II-2501, paragraph 177, and Case T-112/07 Hitachi and Others v Commission [2011] ECR II-3871, paragraph 58).

63 In the latter situation, it is necessary to take account of the principle of the presumption of innocence resulting in particular from Article 6(2) of the European Convention for the Protection of Human Rights and Fundamental Freedoms (ECHR), signed in Rome on 4 November 1950, and from Article 47 of the Charter of Fundamental Rights of the European Union. Given the nature of the infringements in question and the nature and degree of severity of the ensuing penalties, the principle of the presumption of innocence applies in particular to the procedures relating to infringements of the competition rules applicable to undertakings that may result in the imposition of fines or periodic penalty payments (Case C-199/92 P Hüls v Commission [1999] ECR I-4287, paragraphs 149 and 150; and Case C-235/92 P Montecatini v Commission [1999] ECR I-4539, paragraphs 175 and 176; JFE, paragraph 62 above, paragraph 178).

64 Although the Commission must produce sufficiently precise and consistent evidence to support the firm conviction that the alleged infringement took place, it is important to emphasise that it is not necessary for every item of evidence produced by the Commission to satisfy those criteria in relation to every aspect of the infringement. It is sufficient if the body of evidence relied on by the institution, viewed as a whole, meets that requirement, as held by the case-law concerning the implementation of Article 81 EC (see, to that effect Joined Cases C-238/99 P, C-244/99 P, C-245/99 P, C-247/99 P, C-250/99 P to C-252/99 P and C-254/99 P Limburgse Vinyl Maatschappij and Others v Commission [2002] ECR I-8375, paragraphs 513 to 523). That principle applies also in cases concerning the implementation of Article 82 EC (Case T-321/05 AstraZeneca v Commission [2010] ECR II-2805 ('AstraZeneca'), paragraph 477).

65 With respect to the probative force of the evidence used by the Commission, a distinction should be drawn between two situations.

66 First, where the Commission finds that there has been an infringement of the competition rules on the basis that the established facts cannot be explained other than by the existence of anti-competitive behaviour, the Courts of the European Union will find it necessary to annul the decision in question where those undertakings put forward arguments which cast the facts established by the Commission in a different light and thus allow another plausible explanation of the facts to be substituted for the one adopted by the Commission in concluding that an infringement occurred. In such a case, it cannot be considered that the Commission has adduced proof of an infringement of competition law (see, to that effect, Joined Cases 29/83 and 30/83 Compagnie royale asturienne des mines and Rheinzink v Commission [1984] ECR 1679, paragraph 16, and Joined Cases C-89/95, C-104/85, C-114/85, C-116/85, C-117/85 and C-125/85 to C-129/85 Ahlström Osakeyhtiö and Others v Commission [1993] ECR I-1307, paragraphs 126 and 127).

67 Second, when the Commission relies on evidence which is in principle sufficient to demonstrate the existence of the infringement, it is not sufficient for the undertaking concerned to raise the possibility that a circumstance arose which might affect the probative value of that evidence in order for the Commission to bear the burden of proving that that circumstance was not capable of affecting the probative value of that evidence. On the contrary, except in cases where such proof could not be provided by the undertaking concerned on account of the conduct of the Commission itself, it is for the undertaking concerned to prove to the requisite legal standard, on the one hand, the existence of the circumstance relied on by it and, on the other, that that circumstance calls in question the probative value of the evidence relied on by the Commission (see, to that effect, Case T-141/08 E.ON Energie v Commission [2010] ECR II-5761, paragraph 56 and the case-law cited).

68 It is in the light of the foregoing considerations that it is necessary to consider whether the Commission proved to the requisite legal standard the circumstances relied on in the contested decision in the light of the applicant's pleas.

2. The legal characterisation of the rebates and payments in consideration of exclusive supply

69 At recital 924 of the contested decision, the Commission found that the level of the rebates granted to Dell, HP, NEC and Lenovo was de facto conditional upon those companies purchasing all or almost all of their x86 CPU requirements, at least in a certain segment, from Intel and that, consequently, those undertakings' freedom to choose was restricted. As regards the payments granted to MSH, the Commission found, at the same recital, that those payments were conditional upon MSH selling only PCs based on Intel x86 CPUs and that they thereby restricted MSH's freedom to choose. The Commission stated, at recital 925 of the contested decision that, in the absence of objective justification, those findings are sufficient to establish an infringement of Article 82 EC.

70 The applicant contests the Commission's legal characterisation of the payments granted. The applicant maintains in essence that the Commission was required to carry out an assessment of all the surrounding circumstances to see whether the rebates and payments complained of were capable of restricting competition. Before finding that the grant of a rebate is contrary to Article 82 EC, the Commission must prove that those rebates are actually capable of foreclosing competition to the detriment of consumers. Where the conduct is historic, the Commission must prove that the agreements complained of actually led to the foreclosure of competitors.

71 The Commission maintains that the rebates at issue amounted to 'fidelity rebates within the meaning of Hoffmann-La Roche' as resulting from Case 85/76 Hoffmann-La Roche v Commission [1979] ECR 461 ('Hoffmann-La Roche'). It contends that, for this type of practice, it is not necessary to establish actual or potential foreclosure effects on a case-by-case basis.

a) The rebates granted to the OEMs in consideration of exclusive or quasi-exclusive supply

1) Legal characterisation

72 According to settled case-law, an undertaking which is in a dominant position on a market and ties purchasers — even if it does so at their request — by an obligation or promise on their part to obtain all or most of their requirements exclusively from that undertaking abuses its dominant position within the meaning of Article 82 EC, whether the obligation

in question is stipulated without further qualification or whether it is undertaken in consideration of the grant of a rebate (Hoffmann-La Roche, paragraph 71 above, paragraph 89, and Case T-155/06 Tomra Systems and Others v Commission [2010] ECR II-4361 ('Case T-155/06 Tomra'), paragraph 208).

73 The same applies where that undertaking, without tying the purchasers by a formal obligation, applies, either under the terms of agreements concluded with these purchasers or unilaterally, a system of loyalty rebates, that is to say, discounts conditional on the customer's obtaining — whether the quantity of its purchases is large or small — all or most of its requirements from the undertaking in a dominant position (Hoffmann-La Roche, paragraph 71 above, paragraph 89, and Case C-549/10 P Tomra Systems and Others v Commission [2012] ECR ('Case C-549/10 P Tomra'), paragraph 70).

74 As regards in particular whether the grant of a rebate by an undertaking in a dominant position can be characterised as abusive, a distinction should be drawn between three categories of rebates (see, to that effect, Case 322/81 Nederlandsche Banden-Industrie-Michelin v Commission [1983] ECR 3461 ('Michelin I'), paragraphs 71 to 73, and Case C-95/04 P British Airways v Commission [2007] ECR I-2331 ('Case C-95/04 P British Airways'), paragraphs 62, 63, 65, 67 and 68).

75 First, quantity rebate systems ('quantity rebates') linked solely to the volume of purchases made from an undertaking occupying a dominant position are generally considered not to have the foreclosure effect prohibited by Article 82 EC. If increasing the quantity supplied results in lower costs for the supplier, the latter is entitled to pass on that reduction to the customer in the form of a more favourable tariff. Quantity rebates are therefore deemed to reflect gains in efficiency and economies of scale made by the undertaking in a dominant position (see Case T-203/01 Michelin v Commission [2003] ECR II-4071 ('Michelin II'), paragraph 58 and the case-law cited).

76 Second, there are rebates the grant of which is conditional on the customer's obtaining all or most of its requirements from the undertaking in a dominant position. That type of rebate, to which the Commission refers by the expression 'fidelity rebates within the meaning of Hoffmann-La Roche', will subsequently be referred to as 'exclusivity rebates'. It should be noted that that expression will also be used for rebates which are not

conditional on exclusive supply but on the customer's obtaining most of its requirements from the undertaking in a dominant position.

77 Such exclusivity rebates, when applied by an undertaking in a dominant position, are incompatible with the objective of undistorted competition within the common market, because they are not based — save in exceptional circumstances — on an economic transaction which justifies this burden or benefit but are designed to remove or restrict the purchaser's freedom to choose his sources of supply and to deny other producers access to the market (see, to that effect, Hoffmann-La Roche, paragraph 71 above, paragraph 90, and Case T-155/06 Tomra, paragraph 72 above, paragraph 209). Such rebates are designed, through the grant of a financial advantage, to prevent customers from obtaining their supplies from competing producers (Hoffmann-La Roche, paragraph 71 above, paragraph 90, and Case T-155/06 Tomra, paragraph 72 above, paragraph 210).

78 Third, there are other rebate systems where the grant of a financial incentive is not directly linked to a condition of exclusive or quasi-exclusive supply from the undertaking in a dominant position, but where the mechanism for granting the rebate may also have a fidelity-building effect ('rebates falling within the third category'). That category of rebates includes inter alia rebate systems depending on the attainment of individual sales objectives which do not constitute exclusivity rebates, since those systems do not contain any obligation to obtain all or a given proportion of supplies from the dominant undertaking. In examining whether the application of such a rebate constitutes an abuse of dominant position, it is necessary to consider all the circumstances, particularly the criteria and rules governing the grant of the rebate, and to investigate whether, in providing an advantage not based on any economic service justifying it, that rebate tends to remove or restrict the buyer's freedom to choose his sources of supply, to bar competitors from access to the market, or to strengthen the dominant position by distorting competition (see, to that effect, Michelin I, paragraph 74 above, paragraph 73; Case C-95/04 P British Airways, paragraph 74 above, paragraphs 65 and 67; and Case C-549/10 P Tomra, paragraph 73 above, paragraph 71).

79 The rebates granted to Dell, HP, NEC and Lenovo to which the Commission referred, in particular in Article 1(a) to (d) of the contested decision, are rebates falling within the second category, namely exclusivity

rebates. According to the Commission's findings set out in the contested decision, those rebates were conditional upon customers' purchasing from Intel, at least in a certain segment, either all their x86 CPU requirements, in the case of Dell and Lenovo, or most of their requirements, namely 95% in the case of HP and 80% in the case of NEC.

80 The Court would point out that, contrary to the applicant's claim, the question whether an exclusivity rebate can be categorised as abusive does not depend on an analysis of the circumstances of the case aimed at establishing a potential foreclosure effect.

81 It follows from Hoffmann-La Roche, paragraph 71 above (paragraphs 89 and 90), that that type of rebate constitutes an abuse of a dominant position if there is no objective justification for granting it. The Court of Justice did not require proof of a capacity to restrict competition depending on the circumstances of the case.

82 In addition, it follows from Michelin I, paragraph 74 above, and from Case C-95/04 P British Airways, paragraph 74 above, that it is necessary to assess all the circumstances of the case only in the case of rebates falling within the third category. In paragraph 71 of Michelin I, paragraph 74 above, the Court of Justice drew attention to the case-law according to which a rebate, which by offering customers financial advantages tends to prevent them from obtaining their supplies from competing manufacturers, amounts to an abuse within the meaning of Article 82 EC. Next, the Court held, in paragraph 72 of that judgment, that the rebate system at issue in that case did not amount to a mere quantity discount or to a system containing an obligation to obtain all or a given proportion of supplies from the undertaking in a dominant position. The Court lastly observed, in paragraph 73 of that judgment, that it is 'therefore' necessary to consider all the circumstances, particularly the criteria and rules governing the grant of the rebate.

83 In Case C-95/04 P British Airways, paragraph 74 above, the Court first of all recalled, in paragraph 62, the case-law resulting from Hoffmann-La Roche, paragraph 70 above, and then noted the difference between the facts forming the basis of the latter judgment and those underlying Michelin I, paragraph 74 above, stating, in paragraph 65, that Michelin I concerned discounts which did not contain any obligation on the part of the customers of the undertaking in a dominant position to obtain all or a given proportion of their supplies from that undertaking. Next, the

Court held, in paragraph 67, that it followed from the case-law that it is necessary to consider all the circumstances in order to determine whether an undertaking in a dominant position has abused such a position by applying a system of discounts 'such as that described in paragraph 65 of this judgment'. Lastly, in paragraph 68, the Court held that the need to determine whether discounts can produce an exclusionary effect concerns a system of discounts or bonuses 'which constitute neither quantity discounts or bonuses nor fidelity discounts or bonuses within the meaning of the judgment in Hoffmann-La Roche'.

84 It follows that, according to the case-law, it is only in the case of rebates falling within the third category that it is necessary to assess all the circumstances, and not in the case of exclusivity rebates falling within the second category.

85 That approach can be justified by the fact that exclusivity rebates granted by an undertaking in a dominant position are by their very nature capable of restricting competition.

86 The capability of tying customers to the undertaking in a dominant position is inherent in exclusivity rebates. The grant by an undertaking in a dominant position of a rebate in consideration of a customer's obtaining all or most of its requirements implies that the undertaking in a dominant position grants a financial advantage designed to prevent customers from obtaining their supplies from competing producers. It is therefore not necessary to examine the circumstances of the case in order to determine whether that rebate is designed to prevent customers from obtaining their supplies from competitors.

87 It should moreover be noted that exclusivity rebates granted by an undertaking in a dominant position are by their very nature capable of foreclosing competitors. A financial advantage granted for the purpose of inducing a customer to obtain all or most of its requirements from the undertaking in a dominant position means that that customer has an incentive not to obtain, in respect of the part of its requirements concerned by the exclusivity condition, supplies from competitors of the undertaking in a dominant position.

88 In that context, it should be observed that a foreclosure effect occurs not only where access to the market is made impossible for competitors, but also where that access is made more difficult (see, to that effect, Michelin I,

paragraph 74 above, paragraph 85; Case C-52/09 TeliaSonera Sverige [2011] ECR I-527 ('TeliaSonera'), paragraph 63, and Michelin II, paragraph 75 above, paragraph 244). A financial incentive granted by an undertaking in a dominant position in order to induce a customer not to obtain, in respect of the part of its requirements concerned by the exclusivity condition, supplies from its competitors is by its very nature capable of making access to the market more difficult for those competitors.

89 Although exclusivity conditions may, in principle, have beneficial effects for competition, so that in a normal situation on a competitive market, it is necessary to assess their effects on the market in their specific context (see, to that effect, Case C-234/89 Delimitis [1991] ECR I-935, paragraphs 14 to 27), those considerations cannot be accepted in the case of a market where, precisely because of the dominant position of one of the economic operators, competition is already restricted (see, to that effect, Case C-310/93 P BPB Industries and British Gypsum v Commission [1995] ECR I-865 ('Case C-310/93 P BPB Industries and British Gypsum'), paragraph 11, and the Opinion of Advocate General Léger in that case, points 42 to 45).

90 That approach is justified by the special responsibility that an undertaking in a dominant position has not to allow its conduct to impair genuine undistorted competition in the common market and by the fact that, where an economic operator holds a strong position in the market, exclusive supply conditions in respect of a substantial proportion of purchases by a customer constitute an unacceptable obstacle to access to the market (see, to that effect, Case T-65/89 BPB Industries and British Gypsum v Commission [1993] ECR II-389 ('Case T-65/89 BPB Industries and British Gypsum'), paragraphs 65 to 68). In that case, the exclusivity of supply causes additional interference with the structure of competition on the market. Thus, the concept of abuse in principle includes any obligation to obtain supplies exclusively from an undertaking in a dominant position which benefits that undertaking (see, to that effect, Hoffmann-La Roche, paragraph 71 above, paragraphs 120, 121 and 123, Case C-310/93 P BPB Industries and British Gypsum, paragraph 89 above, paragraph 11, and the Opinion of Advocate General Léger in that case, paragraph 89 above, points 46 and 47).

91 Furthermore, it must also be stated that it is inherent in a strong dominant position, such as that occupied by the applicant, that, for a substantial part of the demand, there are no proper substitutes for the

product supplied by the dominant undertaking. The supplier in a dominant position is thus, to a large extent, an unavoidable trading partner (see, to that effect, Hoffmann-La Roche, paragraph 71 above, paragraph 41; Case C-95/04 P British Airways, paragraph 74 above, paragraph 75; and Case T-155/06 Tomra, paragraph 72 above, paragraph 269). In the present case, the applicant does not contest the findings made in the contested decision that its position on the market during the period of the infringement found in this case was that of an unavoidable trading partner.

92 It follows from the position of unavoidable trading partner that customers will in any event obtain part of their requirements from the undertaking in a dominant position ('the non-contestable share'). The competitor of an undertaking in a dominant position is not therefore in a position to compete for the full supply of a customer, but only for the portion of the demand exceeding the non-contestable share ('the contestable share'). The contestable share is thus the portion of a customer's requirements which can realistically be switched to a competitor of the undertaking in a dominant position in any given period, as the Commission states at recital 1009 of the contested decision. The grant of exclusivity rebates by an undertaking in a dominant position makes it more difficult for a competitor to supply its own goods to customers of that dominant undertaking. If a customer of the undertaking in a dominant position obtains supplies from a competitor by failing to comply with the exclusivity or quasi-exclusivity condition, it risks losing not only the rebates for the units that it switched to that competitor, but the entire exclusivity rebate.

93 In order to submit an attractive offer, it is not therefore sufficient for the competitor of an undertaking in a dominant position to offer attractive conditions for the units that that competitor can itself supply to the customer; it must also offer that customer compensation for the loss of the exclusivity rebate. In order to submit an attractive offer, the competitor must therefore apportion the rebate that the undertaking in a dominant position grants in respect of all or almost all of the customer's requirements, including the non-contestable share, to the contestable share alone. Thus, the grant of an exclusivity rebate by an unavoidable trading partner makes it structurally more difficult for a competitor to submit an offer at an attractive price and thus gain access to the market. The grant of exclusivity rebates enables the undertaking in a dominant position to use its economic power on the non-contestable share of the demand of the customer as leverage to secure also

the contestable share, thus making access to the market more difficult for a competitor.

94 Lastly, it should be noted that it is open to the dominant undertaking to justify the use of an exclusivity rebate system, in particular by showing that its conduct is objectively necessary or that the potential foreclosure effect that it brings about may be counterbalanced, outweighed even, by advantages in terms of efficiency that also benefit consumers (see, to that effect, Hoffmann-La Roche, paragraph 71 above, paragraph 90; Case C-95/04 P British Airways, paragraph 74 above, paragraphs 85 and 86; and Case C-209/10 Post Danmark [2012] ECR ('Post Danmark'), paragraphs 40 and 41 and the case-law cited). However, in the case in point, the applicant has put forward no argument in that regard.

2) The applicant's arguments

2.1) The arguments that the Commission is required to carry out an analysis of the circumstances of the case in order to establish at least a potential foreclosure effect

95 The applicant claims that the Commission is required to carry out an analysis of the circumstances of the case in order to establish at least a potential foreclosure effect.

96 First, the applicant relies on paragraph 73 of Michelin I, paragraph 74 above, and on paragraph 67 of Case C-95/04 P British Airways, paragraph 74 above. However, those paragraphs concern rebates falling within the third category and are therefore not relevant so far as concerns exclusivity rebates.

97 In that regard, it is necessary to reject the applicant's argument, raised at the hearing, that the Court of Justice abandoned the distinction between exclusivity rebates and rebates falling within the third category in Case C-549/10 P Tomra, paragraph 73 above. It is true that, in paragraph 70 of that judgment, the Court initially recalled what was stated in paragraph 73 above, namely that the application of a system of loyalty rebates by an undertaking in a dominant position constitutes an abuse, then added, in paragraph 71, that, '[i]n that regard, it is necessary to consider all the circumstances ...'. However, as the Commission rightly observed, it is apparent from the context of the judgment that, in so doing, the Court did not extend the scope of the analysis of the circumstances of the case to exclusivity rebates. The considerations set out in paragraphs 70 and 71

of that judgment in which the Court recalled the case-law are to be found in the examination of the third plea, which did not concern an exclusivity rebate system, but a rebate system falling within the third category, namely a system of individualised retroactive rebates (Case C-549/10 P Tomra, paragraph 73 above, paragraphs 73, 74, 77 and 78, and the Opinion of Advocate General Mazák in that case, point 27).

98 Second, the applicant relies on Case C-280/08 P Deutsche Telekom v Commission [2010] ECR I-9555 ('Case C-280/08 P Deutsche Telekom'), paragraph 175, TeliaSonera, paragraph 88 above, paragraph 28, and Post Danmark, paragraph 94 above, paragraph 26. In those judgments, the Court of Justice held that, 'in order to determine whether the undertaking in a dominant position has abused such a position by its pricing practices, it is necessary to consider all the circumstances ...'.

99 However, the scope of that case-law is limited to pricing practices and does not affect the legal characterisation of exclusivity rebates. Case C-280/08 P Deutsche Telekom, paragraph 98 above, and TeliaSonera, paragraph 88 above, concerned margin squeeze practices and Post Danmark, paragraph 94 above, concerned low price practices, so that those three cases concerned pricing practices. However, the present case does not relate to a pricing practice. As regards the rebates granted to the various OEMs, the complaint made against the applicant in the contested decision is not based on the exact amount of the rebates and thus on the prices charged by the applicant, but on the fact that the grant of those rebates was conditional on exclusive or quasi-exclusive supply. Different treatment of exclusivity rebates and pricing practices is justified by the fact that, unlike an exclusive supply incentive, the level of a price cannot be regarded as unlawful in itself.

100 In that regard, it is also necessary to reject the applicant's argument, put forward at the hearing, that Post Danmark, paragraph 94 above, deals with loyalty rebates comparable to those of the case in point. In that case, the proceedings before the Court of Justice concerned the practice of Post Danmark of charging its main competitor's former customers rates different from those that it charged its own pre-existing customers without being able to justify those significant differences in its rate and rebate conditions by considerations relating to its costs, a practice described by the Danish Competition Authority as 'primary-line price discrimination' (Post Danmark, paragraph 94 above, paragraph 8). That presentation of the anti-

competitive practices contains no reference to an exclusivity rebate system. On the contrary, the proceedings which gave rise to the reference for a preliminary ruling concerned solely whether there was an abuse by means of selectively low prices (Post Danmark, paragraph 94 above, paragraphs 15 to 17). Thus, in reply to the question referred to it for a preliminary ruling, the Court only replied to the question in which circumstances a policy of charging low prices had to be considered to amount to an exclusionary abuse, contrary to Article 82 EC (Post Danmark, paragraph 94 above, paragraph 19).

101 The applicant's arguments must therefore be rejected.

2.2) The argument that the Commission is required to prove actual foreclosure effects

102 The applicant submits that, where the conduct at issue is historic, the Commission is required to prove actual foreclosure effects. The Commission was wrong not to take into account the absence of actual anti-competitive effects of the applicant's practices. Moreover, the applicant maintains that the Commission must establish a causal link between the practices complained of and effects on the market.

103 First of all, it must be stated that, even in the context of an analysis of the circumstances of the case, the Commission must only show that a practice is capable of restricting competition (see, to that effect, Case C-549/10 P Tomra, paragraph 73 above, paragraph 68, and TeliaSonera, paragraph 88 above, paragraph 64). The mechanism of an exclusivity rebate granted by an undertaking in a dominant position which is an unavoidable trading partner enables it to use the non-contestable share of the demand of the customer as leverage to secure also the contestable share (see paragraph 93 above). When such a trading instrument exists, it is unnecessary to undertake an analysis of the actual effects of the rebates on competition (see, to that effect, Case C-549/10 P Tomra, paragraph 73 above, paragraph 79).

104 Next, given that it is not necessary to prove actual effects of the rebates, it follows necessarily from this that the Commission is also not required to prove a causal link between the practices complained of and actual effects on the market. Thus, the circumstance claimed by the applicant that customers bought exclusively from it for business reasons which were entirely independent of the rebates, assuming that it were proved, does not

mean that those rebates were not capable of inducing customers to obtain their supplies exclusively from it.

105 Lastly, the Court would point out that, a fortiori, the Commission is not required to prove either direct damage to consumers or a causal link between such damage and the practices at issue in the contested decision. It is apparent from the case-law that Article 82 EC is aimed not only at practices which may cause damage to consumers directly, but also at those which are detrimental to them through their impact on an effective competition structure (Case C-95/04 P British Airways, paragraph 74 above, paragraph 106).

2.3) The argument alleging absence of formal obligations

106 The applicant maintains that the rebates at issue in the present case did not involve formal or binding exclusivity obligations. However, it follows from Hoffmann-La Roche, paragraph 71 above (paragraph 89), that an undertaking in a dominant position abuses that position if it applies an exclusivity rebate system even 'without tying the purchasers by a formal obligation'. In that regard, the Commission correctly states that the anti-competitive incentive of exclusivity rebates results not from the imposition of a formal obligation to buy exclusively or almost exclusively from the dominant company but from the financial advantages obtained or the financial disadvantages avoided by making such purchases. Thus, it is sufficient that the undertaking in a dominant position indicates in a credible manner to its customer that the grant of a financial advantage depends on exclusive or quasi-exclusive supply.

2.4) The argument alleging the relevance of the amount of the rebate

107 The applicant states that the Commission failed to take account of the level of the rebates granted by Intel to the OEMs in return for exclusive or quasi-exclusive supply and that it is illogical to censure very small rebates (USD 1 for example) that AMD would have been able to exceed.

108 However, as the Commission correctly observes, it is not the level of the rebates which is at issue in the contested decision but the exclusivity for which they were given. Thus, the rebate must only be capable of inducing the customer to purchase exclusively, irrespective whether the competing

supplier could have compensated the customer for the loss of the rebate if that customer switched supplier.

109 It is not therefore necessary to consider the question whether, in the purely theoretical example of a rebate in an amount of USD 1 only as put forward by the applicant, such a minimum rebate is capable of constituting an incentive for the customer to comply with the exclusivity condition. In the case in point, the Commission proved to the requisite legal standard that the applicant had granted rebates to the OEMs amounting to millions of USD annually. The Commission moreover proved to the requisite legal standard that those rebates were granted, at least in part, in consideration of exclusivity (see paragraphs 444 to 584, 673 to 798, 900 to 1017, 1145 to 1208 and 1381 to 1502 below). Those matters suffice to show that the exclusivity rebates at issue in the contested decision were capable of inducing the OEMs to purchase exclusively.

2.5) The argument based on the relevance of the duration

110 In the applicant's submission, account must be taken of the short duration of its supply contracts and of the fact that some of those contracts could be terminated at 30 days' notice.

111 That argument must also be rejected. In that regard, it must be borne in mind that, in principle, any financial incentive to purchase exclusively constitutes additional interference with the structure of competition on a market and must therefore be regarded as abusive to the extent that it is implemented by an undertaking in a dominant position (see paragraph 90 above).

112 As regards the argument based on the possibility of terminating certain contracts at short notice, the Court would point out that the right to terminate a contract in no way prevents its actual application until such time as the right to terminate it has been exercised (Case T-65/89 BPB Industries and British Gypsum, paragraph 90 above, paragraph 73).

113 Moreover, it should be noted that, in the present case, for all the OEMs and for MSH, the total period during which exclusivity rebates were applied was not short. That period lasted from approximately one year, in the case of Lenovo, to more than five years, in the case of MSH. In that context, it must be stated that the incentive for customers to purchase all or almost all of their requirements from the undertaking in a dominant position continues to exist for as long as the latter grants exclusivity rebates, irrespective of

whether a long-term contract has been concluded or whether there is a succession of several short-term contracts (see, also, paragraph 195 below).

2.6) The argument based on the small part of the market concerned by the conduct complained of

114 The applicant claims that the Commission ought to have taken into consideration the fact that the practices at issue in the contested decision concerned only a small part of the x86 CPU market, namely between 0.3% and 2% per year.

115 It should be observed as a preliminary point that, for the reasons which will be set out in paragraphs 187 to 194 below, such an argument has no factual basis, since the calculation method used by the applicant to reach those figures is erroneous.

116 In addition, the possible smallness of the parts of the market which are concerned by the practices at issue is not a relevant argument. Where the course of conduct under consideration is that of an undertaking occupying a dominant position on a market where for this reason the structure of competition has already been weakened, any further weakening of the structure of competition may constitute an abuse of a dominant position (Hoffmann-La Roche, paragraph 71 above, paragraph 123). The Court of Justice has therefore rejected the application of an 'appreciable effect' criterion or a de minimis threshold for the purposes of applying Article 82 EC (Opinion of Advocate General Mazák in Case C-549/10 P Tomra, paragraph 73 above, point 17).

117 Furthermore, the customers on the foreclosed part of the market should have the opportunity to benefit from whatever degree of competition is possible on the market and competitors should be able to compete on the merits for the entire market and not just for a part of it (Case C-549/10 P Tomra, paragraph 73 above, paragraphs 42 and 46). A dominant undertaking may not therefore justify the grant of exclusivity rebates to certain customers by the fact that competitors remain free to supply other customers.

118 It follows that the applicant's line of argument must be rejected.

119 That conclusion is not undermined by the fact that, in Case C-549/10 P Tomra, paragraph 73 above (paragraphs 41 to 45), the Court of Justice approved the General Court's reasoning that the part of the market

which had been foreclosed in that case was 'significant'. That reasoning does not confirm the proposition that there can be no foreclosure effect where the foreclosed part of the market is not significant. In that regard, it should be noted that, according to Case T-155/06 Tomra, paragraph 72 above (paragraph 243), the General Court found that 'even accepting the applicants' proposition that foreclosure of a small portion of demand does not matter, that portion was far from being small in the present case'. The General Court did not therefore adopt a position on whether that proposition was correct.

120 It was sufficient for the Court of Justice to approve the finding of the General Court that, in that case, a significant part of the market had been foreclosed, without that being understood as meaning that the Court of Justice took the view that the foreclosure of a significant part of the market was a necessary condition for the finding of an abuse. Moreover, the Court of Justice expressly held, in Case C-549/10 P Tomra, paragraph 73 above (paragraph 46), that the determination of a precise threshold of foreclosure of the market beyond which the practices at issue had to be regarded as abusive was not required for the purposes of applying Article 82 EC and that, 'in any event', it had been proved to the requisite legal standard that the market had been closed to competition by the practices at issue.

121 That conclusion is also not undermined by Case T-65/98 Van den Bergh Foods v Commission [2003] ECR II-4653, paragraph 160, which is relied upon by the applicant and ACT. That judgment did not concern a practice by which a financial incentive was directly conditional on the customer's obtaining all or most of its requirements from the undertaking in a dominant position. In that case, the undertaking in a dominant position had supplied Irish ice-cream retailers with freezer cabinets free of charge, provided that they be used exclusively to stock ice creams supplied by the undertaking in a dominant position. However, the retailers remained free to sell ice creams supplied by competitors if they stocked them in their own freezer cabinets or in freezer cabinets made available by other ice-cream manufacturers.

122 It was in those circumstances that the Commission took the view that it was an abuse of a dominant position for the undertaking in a dominant position to induce retailers in Ireland not having a freezer cabinet either procured by themselves or provided by another ice-cream manufacturer to enter into freezer-cabinet agreements subject to a condition of exclusivity

by offering to supply to them one or more freezer cabinets for the stocking of single-wrapped items of impulse ice-cream, and to maintain the cabinets, free of any direct charge (Van den Bergh Foods v Commission, paragraph 121 above, paragraph 23). The Commission also found, in that case, that in some 40% of all outlets in Ireland the only freezer cabinet/s for the storage of impulse ice-cream in place in the outlet was or were provided by the undertaking in a dominant position (Van den Bergh Foods v Commission, paragraph 121 above, paragraph 19).

123 It was in those circumstances that the General Court held, in Van den Bergh Foods v Commission, paragraph 121 above (paragraph 160), that '[t]he fact that an undertaking in a dominant position on a market ties de facto — even at their own request — 40% of outlets in the relevant market by an exclusivity clause which in reality creates outlet exclusivity constitutes an abuse of a dominant position'.

124 It should be observed that, in that case, it was only in respect of those 40% of outlets that the condition that only products supplied by the undertaking in a dominant position could be stocked operated de facto as an exclusivity condition, since the other outlets had at their disposal other freezer cabinets in which they could stock ice creams supplied by other manufacturers. It cannot therefore be inferred from that judgment that, for rebates which are directly linked to an exclusive or quasi-exclusive supply condition, it is necessary to determine the share of the market which is foreclosed.

2.7) The argument that the alleged exclusivity conditions did not cover a significant portion of certain OEMs' requirements

125 The applicant states that, as regards certain OEMs, namely HP, NEC and Lenovo, the exclusivity condition found by the Commission in the contested decision did not concern the entire x86 CPU demand of those OEMs, but, in the case of HP, only 95% of its corporate desktop x86 CPU requirements, in the case of NEC, only 80% of its 'client' PC x86 CPU requirements, namely desktop computers and notebook computers, with the exception of servers, and, in the case of Lenovo, only its notebook x86 CPU requirements.

126 At the hearing, the applicant added that HP's x86 CPU corporate desktop requirements amounted to only 30% of HP's total x86 CPU requirements. Since the alleged condition covered only 95% of HP's

corporate desktop x86 CPU requirements, that condition concerned only approximately 28% of HP's total x86 CPU requirements and could not therefore be regarded as an exclusivity condition.

127 By that argument, the applicant claims in essence that the rebates granted to HP, NEC and Lenovo cannot be regarded as exclusivity rebates, since the condition did not concern 'all or most', within the meaning of Hoffmann-La Roche, paragraph 71 above (paragraph 89), of those OEMs' x86 CPU requirements.

128 That line of argument must be rejected.

129 With respect to the rebates granted to HP, it should be noted that the conduct at issue is not linked to the condition that HP was required to purchase at least 28% of its total x86 CPU requirements from Intel, but to the condition that HP was required to purchase, in a certain segment of the market, 95% of its total x86 CPU requirements from Intel. The condition that HP was required to purchase, in a given sector, 95% of its requirements from the undertaking in a dominant position is neither identical to nor comparable to a hypothetical condition according to which HP was required to purchase 28% of its requirements in all segments from Intel.

130 HP's freedom to obtain its corporate desktop x86 CPU requirements from AMD was liable to be limited on account of the exclusivity rebates granted by Intel. If HP had decided to purchase more than 5% of its corporate desktop x86 CPU requirements from AMD and thus not to comply with the quasi-exclusivity condition, it would have risked losing the exclusivity rebate, and not only in respect of the units purchased from AMD. Thus, in order to be able to supply more than 5% of HP's corporate desktop x86 CPU requirements, AMD would not only have had to make a more attractive offer for x86 CPUs in respect of the contestable share of HP's demand, but also compensate HP for the loss of the exclusivity rebate. That is precisely the anti-competitive mechanism of exclusivity rebates.

131 That mechanism was not neutralised by the fact that AMD was able to supply HP with its x86 CPU requirements in respect of all consumer computers and in respect of corporate notebook computers. The fact that HP's freedom of choice was not limited in those segments of the market does not call in question the fact that HP's freedom of choice was liable to be limited in the corporate desktop segment.

132 In that context, it should be recalled that competitors of the undertaking in a dominant position must be able to compete on the merits for the entire market and not just for a part of it (Case C-549/10 P Tomra, paragraph 73 above, paragraph 42). An undertaking in a dominant position may not therefore justify the grant of exclusivity rebates to certain customers by the fact that its competitors are free to supply other customers (see paragraph 117 above). Similarly, an undertaking in a dominant position may not justify the grant of a rebate subject to a quasi-exclusive purchase condition by a customer in a certain segment of a market by the fact that that customer remains free to obtain supplies from competitors in other segments.

133 In that context, it is of no relevance that — as argued by ACT at the hearing — when defining the relevant product market, the Commission did not draw a distinction between CPUs used in corporate computers and consumer computers, as is apparent from recital 831(2) of the contested decision. The anti-competitive mechanism of the exclusivity rebates which were applied in the present case operates irrespective of whether or not the CPUs used in corporate computers and consumer computers are interchangeable. In the present case, the condition was stipulated in relation to HP's corporate desktop requirements. HP was therefore required to use Intel CPUs in 95% of corporate desktops containing x86 CPUs that it produced. The question whether those CPUs are different from the x86 CPUs used for consumer computers is irrelevant in that context since, even if they were interchangeable, HP would not have been able to use competitors' CPUs in more than 5% of its corporate desktops without infringing the condition of the exclusivity rebate.

134 It follows that the rebates granted to HP must be regarded as exclusivity rebates, even though the quasi-exclusivity condition concerned only a segment of HP's requirements.

135 As regards the rebates granted to NEC, it must be observed that the percentage of 80% covered by the exclusivity condition is sufficient to constitute 'most' of its requirements within the meaning of Hoffmann-La Roche, paragraph 71 above (paragraph 89). In that context, it should be noted that, in that judgment, the conduct in question included purchasing obligations concerning inter alia 80% or 75% of a customer's requirements (Hoffmann-La Roche, paragraph 71 above, paragraph 83).

136 The fact that the exclusivity condition concerned only desktop computers and notebook computers, with the exception of servers, is irrelevant. In that regard, the points made in paragraphs 130 to 132 above apply mutatis mutandis.

137 Lastly, with respect to the rebates granted to Lenovo, the fact that the exclusivity condition concerned only notebook computers is irrelevant for the same reasons.

2.8) The argument based on customers' buying power

138 The applicant states that customers' buying power precludes the abuse. In the present case, customers used their buying power as leverage to obtain larger rebates.

139 That argument must be rejected. The claim — even if it were established — that the rebates granted by the applicant represented a response to requests and to customers' buying power does not justify making them subject to an exclusive supply condition (see, to that effect, Hoffmann-La Roche, paragraph 71 above, paragraph 89; Case T-65/89 BPB Industries and British Gypsum, paragraph 90 above, paragraph 68; and Case T-66/01 Imperial Chemical Industries v Commission [2010] ECR II-2631, paragraph 305). As the Court of Justice held in Hoffmann-La Roche, paragraph 71 above (paragraph 120), the fact that the dominant undertaking's contracting partner is itself a powerful undertaking and that the contract is clearly not the outcome of pressure brought to bear by the dominant undertaking on its partner does not preclude the existence of an abuse of a dominant position, since such an abuse consists in the additional interference, due to the obligation to obtain supplies exclusively, with the structure of competition in a market in which in consequence of the presence there of an undertaking occupying a dominant position the degree of competition has already been weakened. Moreover, the OEMs' buying power does not alter the fact that they depended on the applicant as an unavoidable trading partner in the x86 CPU market.

2.9) The line of argument concerning the relevance of the AEC test

140 The applicant submits that the AEC test (see paragraph 30 above) is an important factor when establishing the potential foreclosure effect of the rebates at issue. The AEC test is the only evidence that the Commission

presented in the contested decision to show that Intel's rebates were capable of causing anti-competitive foreclosure. However, the Commission disputes that the AEC test forms part of the legal analysis of the contested decision. It follows, in the applicant's submission, that the legal assessment carried out by the Commission in the contested decision failed to establish the foreclosure capability of the rebates at issue. Moreover, in the applicant's submission, the Commission made numerous errors in applying that test. In its submission, proper application of the AEC test demonstrates that the rebates granted by Intel did not have a foreclosure capability.

141 It should be observed as a preliminary point that the AEC test carried out in the contested decision takes as a starting point the circumstance, noted in paragraph 93 above, that an as-efficient competitor, which seeks to obtain the contestable share of the orders hitherto satisfied by a dominant undertaking which is an unavoidable trading partner, must compensate the customer for the exclusivity rebate that it would lose if it purchased a smaller portion than that stipulated by the exclusivity or quasi-exclusivity condition. The AEC test is designed to determine whether the competitor which is as efficient as the undertaking in a dominant position, which faces the same costs as the latter, can still cover its costs in that case.

142 As regards the relevance of the AEC test with respect to exclusivity rebates, the Court makes the following observations.

143 First of all, it should be recalled that a finding that an exclusivity rebate is illegal does not necessitate an examination of the circumstances of the case (see paragraphs 80 to 93 above). The Commission is not therefore required to demonstrate the foreclosure capability of exclusivity rebates on a case-by-case basis.

144 Next, it follows from the case-law that, even in the case of rebates falling within the third category, for which an examination of the circumstances of the case is necessary, it is not essential to carry out an AEC test. Thus, in Michelin I, paragraph 74 above (paragraphs 81 to 86), the Court of Justice relied on the loyalty mechanism of the rebates at issue, without requiring proof, by means of a quantitative test, that competitors had been forced to sell at a loss in order to be able to compensate the rebates falling within the third category granted by the undertaking in a dominant position.

145 Moreover, it follows from Case C-549/10 P Tomra, paragraph 73 above (paragraphs 73 and 74), that, in order to find anti-competitive effects, it is

not necessary that a rebate system force an as-efficient competitor to charge 'negative' prices, that is to say prices lower than the cost price. In order to establish a potential anti-competitive effect, it is sufficient to demonstrate the existence of a loyalty mechanism (see, to that effect, Case C-549/10 P Tomra, paragraph 73 above, paragraph 79).

146 It follows that, even if an assessment of the circumstances of the case were necessary to demonstrate the potential anti-competitive effects of the exclusivity rebates, it would still not be necessary to demonstrate those effects by means of an AEC test.

147 Moreover, the applicant's argument that the AEC test is the only evidence that the Commission presented in the contested decision in order to demonstrate the foreclosure capability of the rebates at issue has no factual basis (see paragraphs 173 to 175 below).

148 With respect to the applicant's argument that it would have demonstrated by means of an AEC test carried out properly that the rebates at issue did not have a foreclosure capability, the Court makes the following observations.

149 First of all, it should be borne in mind that a foreclosure effect occurs not only where access to the market is made impossible for competitors. Indeed, it is sufficient that that access be made more difficult (see paragraph 88 above).

150 However, it must be stated that an AEC test only makes it possible to verify the hypothesis that access to the market has been made impossible and not to rule out the possibility that it has been made more difficult. It is true that a negative result means that it is economically impossible for an as-efficient competitor to secure the contestable share of a customer's demand. In order to offer a customer compensation for the loss of the exclusivity rebate, that competitor would be forced to sell its products at a price which would not allow it even to cover its costs. However, a positive result means only that an as-efficient competitor is able to cover its costs (in the case of the AEC test as carried out in the contested decision and proposed by the applicant, only the average avoidable costs). That does not however mean that there is no foreclosure effect. The mechanism of the exclusivity rebates, as described in paragraph 93 above, is still capable of making access to the market more difficult for competitors of the undertaking in a dominant position, even if that access is not economically impossible (see, as regards

that distinction, point 54 of the Opinion of Advocate General Mazák in Case C-549/10 P Tomra, paragraph 73 above).

151 It follows from the foregoing that it is not necessary to consider whether the Commission carried out the AEC test in accordance with the applicable rules and that it is also not necessary to examine the question whether the alternative calculations proposed by the applicant were carried out correctly. Even a positive AEC test result would not be capable of ruling out the potential foreclosure effect which is inherent in the mechanism described in paragraph 93 above.

152 That conclusion is not undermined by TeliaSonera, paragraph 88 above, Case C-280/08 P Deutsche Telekom, paragraph 98 above, and Post Danmark, paragraph 94 above. The applicant submits that it follows from those judgments that the key criterion is whether a competitor as efficient as the dominant undertaking could continue to compete with the dominant undertaking. However, it should be borne in mind that those cases concerned margin squeeze practices (TeliaSonera and Deutsche Telekom) or low price practices (Post Danmark). The obligation resulting from those judgments to carry out price and cost analyses is attributable to the fact that it is impossible to assess whether a price is abusive without comparing it with other prices and costs. A price cannot be unlawful in itself. However, in the case of an exclusivity rebate, it is the condition of exclusive or quasi-exclusive supply to which its grant is subject rather than the amount of the rebate which makes it abusive.

153 Moreover, it follows from Case C-549/10 P Tomra, paragraph 73 above (paragraphs 73, 74 and 80), which postdates the judgments cited in the previous paragraph, that it is not essential to examine whether a rebate system forces an as-efficient competitor to charge negative prices, even in the case of rebates falling within the third category. A fortiori, it is not necessary to do so as regards exclusivity rebates.

154 The conclusion is also not undermined by the Communication from the Commission entitled 'Guidance on the Commission's enforcement priorities in applying Article 82 [EC] to abusive exclusionary conduct by dominant undertakings (OJ 2009 C 45 p. 7; 'the Article 82 Guidance').

155 According to paragraph 2 of the Article 82 Guidance, '[t]his document sets out the enforcement priorities that will guide the Commission's action in applying Article 82 [EC]'. As the Commission observed at recital 916

of the contested decision, since the Article 82 Guidance is intended to set priorities for the cases that the Commission will focus upon in the future, it does not apply to proceedings that had already been initiated before it was published. Since the Commission decision to initiate proceedings is dated 26 July 2007, the Commission was not therefore in any event required to follow the Article 82 Guidance in the present case.

156 The fact that the Article 82 Guidance was published before the adoption of the contested decision does not mean that it was applicable. The fact that the Commission provides indications on the enforcement priorities that will guide its action in the future cannot oblige it to reconsider whether it deal with a case as a priority that it had already decided to deal with as a priority and the treatment of which, moreover, is at an advanced stage.

157 It is not therefore necessary to consider whether the contested decision is in line with the Article 82 Guidance.

158 The mere fact that the Commission stated, at recital 916 of the contested decision, that it none the less considered that that decision was in line with the Article 82 Guidance is not capable of calling in question the lack of relevance of the Article 82 Guidance for this case. It is clearly a point that the Commission raised for the sake of completeness, having explained that the Article 82 Guidance was not applicable in the present case.

159 With respect to the circumstance, relied on by the applicant, that the Member of the Commission responsible for competition at the time stated, in a speech of 17 July 2009, that, in the Intel case, the Commission had applied the AEC test in accordance with the methodology set out in the Article 82 Guidance, it should be pointed out that it is clearly apparent from the contested decision, which was adopted by the College of Commissioners, that the Commission considered that the Article 82 Guidance was not applicable and that the AEC test did not constitute a necessary element to show that the practices at issue were illegal. It was therefore for the sake of completeness that the Commission carried out an AEC test and found that the contested decision was in line with the Article 82 Guidance. The fact that the Member of the Commission responsible for competition gave a speech after the adoption of the contested decision, in which that member stated that the Commission had carried out an AEC test in the Intel case, without specifying in that regard that that test had been carried out for the sake of completeness, is not such as to alter the interpretation to be given to the contested decision.

160 In reply to a question put at the hearing, the applicant stated that its reasoning relating to the relevance of the AEC test, which it claims played an important role during the administrative procedure, had to be understood as meaning that it was also relying on the principle of the protection of legitimate expectations.

161 In that regard, it must be recalled that, according to settled case-law, the right to rely on the principle of the protection of legitimate expectations, which is one of the fundamental principles of the European Union, extends to any individual in a situation in which it is clear that the European Union authorities, by giving him precise assurances, have caused him to entertain legitimate expectations. Such assurances, in whatever form they are given, are precise, unconditional and consistent information from authorised and reliable sources. However, a person may not plead breach of the principle unless he has been given precise assurances by the authorities (see Case T-273/01 Innova Privat-Akademie v Commission [2003] ECR II-1093, paragraph 26 and the case-law cited).

162 In the present case, the applicant did not show the existence of a precise assurance given during the administrative procedure that the AEC test was essential for the Commission in order to establish an infringement of Article 82 EC. On the contrary, as the Commission rightly noted at the hearing, according to the second paragraph of Section II 1 of the Final report of the Hearing Officer in this case (OJ 2009 C 227, p. 7), 'during the Hearing the Commission made it clear to Intel, and Intel understood, that the economic assessment was not a condition for a finding of abuse'.

163 The applicant then made it clear, at the hearing, that it had fully understood the Hearing Officer's comments. The applicant claimed that it follows however from point 340 of the Statement of Objections of 2007 that, in the event that proof of a foreclosure capability were necessary, the Commission relies solely on the AEC test in order to prove that capability.

164 It must however be observed that the mere fact that the Commission stated, in point 340 of the Statement of Objections of 2007, that it would establish that the rebates in question had a foreclosure effect, since they prevented an as-efficient competitor from being able to compensate the OEM for the loss in potential rebate, cannot be regarded as a precise assurance that the Commission would not rely on any other ground in order to establish the foreclosure capability. Moreover, it is apparent from points 260 and 329 of the Supplementary Statement of Objections of 2008

that, in its analysis, the Commission did not rely exclusively on the AEC test, but also on other qualitative and quantitative evidence.

165 The Commission did not therefore infringe the principle of the protection of legitimate expectations by the approach that it followed in the contested decision.

166 It follows from the foregoing that the arguments put forward by the applicant are not capable of undermining the conclusion that it is not necessary to consider whether the Commission carried out the AEC test in accordance with the applicable rules or to examine in detail the applicant's arguments regarding the errors that the Commission allegedly made when carrying out that test, or the conclusion that it is also not necessary to examine the alternative calculations proposed by the applicant (see paragraph 151 above).

b) The payments granted to MSH

167 The Commission finds in essence, at recital 1000 of the contested decision, that the effect of the payments granted to MSH on condition that it sell exclusively the applicant's products was equivalent to that of an exclusivity rebate and that those payments therefore fulfilled the conditions laid down by the case-law for qualification as abusive.

168 At the hearing, the applicant claimed in essence that the Commission had wrongly applied the same test for the legal characterisation of the exclusivity rebates granted to the OEMs and for the characterisation of the payments granted to MSH. The applicant submitted inter alia that, unlike the OEMs, MSH was an operator that was present on the retail market. For the purposes of examining whether a competing producer is denied access to the retail market, the applicant claims that the case-law requires an analysis of the cumulative effects produced by a network of exclusive relationships. However, during the period at issue, MSH allegedly held only a very small portion of the relevant worldwide market, namely approximately 1%.

169 It must be stated that the applicant's argument amounts to an assertion that the Commission ought to have carried out an analysis of the circumstances of the case in the retail market in order to demonstrate that the applicant's practices vis-à-vis MSH were capable of restricting competition. However, that argument cannot be accepted. As the Commission rightly observed at the hearing, the anti-competitive mechanism of the applicant's

practices vis-à-vis the OEMs and vis-à-vis MSH was the same, the only difference being that the exclusivity payment granted to MSH was not designed to prevent the supply of a direct customer of the applicant by a competitor, but rather the sale of competing products by a retailer further down the supply chain. OEMs incorporate CPUs in computers that are then sold to consumers by retailers such as MSH. By inducing a retailer to sell computers equipped exclusively with Intel CPUs, the applicant therefore deprived OEMs of a distribution channel for computers equipped with competing undertakings' CPUs. Thus, by depriving MSH of its freedom of choice as regards its sales, it restricted the OEMs' freedom of choice as regards their distribution channels. Given that that restriction was capable of having repercussions for OEMs' demand for AMD CPUs, inducing MSH into an exclusive sale tended to make it more difficult for AMD to gain access to the x86 CPU market. In both situations, the applicant used its economic power on the non-contestable share of the demand as leverage to secure also the contestable share of the demand, thus making access to the market more difficult for AMD (see paragraph 93 above).

170 Whilst it is true that, in the context of Article 81 EC, the Court of Justice has held that, in a normal situation on a competitive market, it is necessary to assess the exclusive relationships between a supplier and a retailer in their specific context, which has implied in particular an analysis of the cumulative effect of a network of such relationships, it is however clear that those considerations cannot be accepted in the context of the implementation of Article 82 EC, which relates to markets in which, precisely because of the dominant position of one of the economic operators, competition is already restricted (see paragraph 89 above).

171 Accordingly, also as regards the payments granted to MSH, the Commission was not required to examine the circumstances of the case, but was required only to demonstrate that the applicant had granted a financial incentive which was subject to an exclusivity condition.

c) Analysis of the capability of the rebates to restrict competition according to the circumstances of the case

172 For the sake of completeness, as regards whether, in the contested decision, the Commission established the capability of the exclusivity rebates and payments granted to Dell, HP, NEC, Lenovo and MSH to

restrict competition also following an analysis of the circumstances of the case, the Court makes the following observations.

173 As a preliminary point, it must be observed that, at recital 924 of the contested decision, the Commission considered that the exclusivity rebates and payments granted to Dell, HP, NEC, Lenovo and MSH were part of a long-term strategy aimed at foreclosing competitors from the market. At recital 925 of the contested decision, the Commission stated that it had demonstrated, in sections VII.4.2.3 to VII.4.2.6 of that decision, that, on top of fulfilling the conditions set out in the case-law, Intel's practices were capable of producing or likely to produce a foreclosure effect. Although not indispensable for establishing an infringement of Article 82 EC, one possible way of showing that Intel's practices were capable of causing or likely to cause foreclosure of competitors is to conduct an as-efficient competitor analysis (see section VII.4.2.3 of the contested decision). On the basis of the results of this analysis and the qualitative and quantitative evidence (see sections VII.4.2.4 and VII.4.2.5 of the contested decision), and given the lack of objective justification and lack of efficiencies (see section VII.4.2.6 of the contested decision), the Commission concluded, at recital 925 of the contested decision, that Intel's conditional rebates to Dell, HP, NEC and Lenovo, as well as Intel's payments to MSH, were an abuse which deserved its particular attention.

174 Moreover, it must be observed that other parts of the contested decision, in particular those concerning the presentation of the products concerned and the conduct at issue in that decision, in sections V and VI of that decision, those concerning the definition of the market, in sections VII.1 and VII.2 of that decision, and the applicant's dominant position, in section VII.3 of that decision, together with the parts concerning the legal characterisation of the exclusivity payments, in section VII.4.2.2 of that decision, must be regarded as the basis of the Commission's conclusion that the payments at issue were capable of restricting competition.

175 Contrary to the applicant's submission, the AEC test is therefore not the only evidence presented in the contested decision in order to demonstrate that the exclusivity payments were capable of restricting competition (see paragraph 147 above).

176 As regards the assessment of the capability of the exclusivity rebates and payments at issue in the present case to restrict competition, it should be noted that, in the context of an analysis of the circumstances of the case,

the Commission must examine, particularly in the light of the criteria and rules governing the grant of the exclusivity payments, whether, in providing an advantage not based on any economic service justifying it, those rebates and payments tend to remove or restrict the buyer's freedom to choose his sources of supply, to bar competitors from access to the market, or to strengthen the dominant position by distorting competition (see, to that effect, Case C-549/10 P Tomra, paragraph 73 above, paragraph 71).

177 It should be made clear that, even in the context of an analysis of the circumstances of the case, the Commission is not required to demonstrate the existence of an actual effect. The Commission may confine itself to establishing that the conduct complained of was capable of restricting competition (see paragraph 103 above).

178 In that regard, it should be observed that, even if the view were to be taken that the grant of an exclusivity rebate or payment by an undertaking in a dominant position is not, in itself, capable of restricting competition, the fact remains that the grant of such a financial incentive by an unavoidable trading partner, such as the applicant, provides at least an indication that it is capable of restricting competition. Where it is granted by an unavoidable trading partner, an exclusivity rebate enables the latter to use its economic power on the non-contestable portion of the demand as leverage to secure also the contestable share, thus making access to the market more difficult for the competitor (see paragraphs 91 and 92 above).

179 That inherent capability of exclusivity rebates and payments to make access to the market more difficult for a competitor is, in the case in point, confirmed by the findings made at recital 893 of the contested decision according to which the rebates were an important element for OEMs to consider on account of the strong competition on the OEM market and their low operating margins. The applicant does not contest those specific characteristics of the market on which the OEMs operate. The particular importance of rebates for their beneficiaries reinforces the incentive for those beneficiaries to comply with the exclusive or quasi-exclusive purchasing conditions and thus contributes to the capability of the rebates to restrict competition.

180 In addition, proof that the financial incentive was indeed taken into consideration by its beneficiaries when deciding to obtain all or almost all of their requirements from the undertaking in a dominant position or not to sell competing products constitutes a factor confirming the

capability of that financial incentive to restrict competition. In the present case, the Commission demonstrated that the exclusivity rebates and payments granted by the applicant were at least a factor that was taken into consideration by Dell, HP, NEC and Lenovo in their decision to obtain all or almost all of their requirements from the applicant, and by MSH in its decision not to sell competing products (see paragraphs 592 to 599, 882 to 890, 1027 to 1030, 1215 to 1220 and 1513 to 1521 below).

181 Moreover, the capability of the exclusivity rebates and payments granted to the four OEMs and to MSH to restrict competition is, in the case in point, confirmed by the findings made in the contested decision, according to which the applicant implemented two different types of abuse, namely, on the one hand, exclusivity rebates and payments and, on the other hand, naked restrictions. As the Commission rightly found at recitals 917, 1681, in conjunction with footnote 1999 (footnote 1990 in the public version), and 1747 of the contested decision, those two types of practices complement and reinforce one another.

182 Furthermore, it should be pointed out that the fact that an undertaking in a dominant position attempts to tie important customers is also a factor which can be taken into account when assessing the anti-competitive nature of its conduct (see, to that effect, Case C-549/10 P Tomra, paragraph 73 above, paragraph 75). It should be noted that, according to the contested decision, Dell and HP in particular can be distinguished from other OEMs by their high market shares, their strong presence in the more profitable segment of the market and their ability to legitimise a new x86 CPU in the market. In the contested decision, the Commission found, at recital 1597, that targeting such undertakings, which are particularly strategically important for market access, has a more significant impact on the overall market than would correspond to their aggregate market share alone, and the applicant did not contest this. Consequently, the Commission was entitled to conclude that the exclusivity rebates concerned important OEMs.

183 With respect to MSH, it will be demonstrated in more detail in paragraphs 1507 to 1511 below that that undertaking was particularly strategically important so far as concerned the distribution of consumer computers equipped with x86 CPUs in Europe.

184 Lastly, it must be stated that the fact that the practices at issue in the contested decision are part of an overall strategy aimed at barring AMD's

access to the most important sales channels is also a circumstance which confirms the capability of the exclusivity rebates and payments to restrict competition (see, to that effect, Case C-549/10 P Tomra, paragraph 73 above, paragraphs 19 and 20). It will be demonstrated in more detail in paragraphs 1523 to 1552 below that the Commission proved the existence of such an overall strategy to the requisite legal standard.

185 First, the applicant attempts to demonstrate that its practices were not capable of restricting competition by arguing that, during the relevant period, AMD reaped the greatest commercial success in its history, reported uniquely rapid growth rates with the very OEMs deemed to be the target of abusive behaviour, faced manufacturing capacity constraints that hampered its ability to satisfy demand for its CPUs and grew its investments in research and development. Moreover, the quality-adjusted price of CPUs fell 36.1% annually over the period covered by the contested decision.

186 Those arguments cannot be accepted. Where an undertaking in a dominant position actually puts into operation practices which are capable of restricting competition, the fact that that capability does not produce actual effects cannot suffice to prevent the application of Article 82 EC (see, to that effect, Case T-219/99 British Airways v Commission [2003] ECR II-5917, paragraph 297). The fact that, over the period covered by the contested decision, AMD reaped great commercial success and, consequently, faced capacity constraints could at most show that the applicant's practices did not produce actual effects. However, that could not suffice to demonstrate that the practices implemented by the applicant were not capable of restricting competition. Moreover, neither the growth in the market shares of AMD and in its research and development investment, nor the decrease in the price of x86 CPUs over the period covered by the contested decision mean that the applicant's practices had no effect. In the absence of those practices, it may legitimately be considered that the increase in the competitor's market share and in its research and development investment and the decrease in the price of x86 CPUs might have been greater (see, to that effect, Michelin II, paragraph 75 above, paragraph 245, and British Airways v Commission, paragraph 298). Consequently, it is not necessary to adjudicate on the Commission's assertions that the applicant's arguments concerning the increase in AMD's market shares and the decrease in the price of x86 CPUs are factually incorrect.

187 Second, the applicant cannot usefully rely on the argument that the practices at issue in the contested decision allegedly concerned only a small part of the global x86 CPU market, namely between 0.3% and 2% per year. In addition to the arguments set out in paragraphs 116 to 124 above, it should be noted that the applicant relies on an erroneous calculation method in order to arrive at the conclusion that its practices affected only between 0.3% and 2% of the x86 CPU market. Those figures were calculated by taking account only of the contestable share (see paragraph 92 above) with respect to the OEMs concerned and MSH and not the entire market share held by those undertakings.

188 Such a calculation method has the effect of artificially reducing the figure arrived at, as the portion of the market which is foreclosed by an exclusivity rebate is not limited to the contestable share. On the contrary, the portion of a customer's requirements which is linked to an exclusivity rebate is foreclosed in its entirety vis-à-vis competitors.

189 It follows that, in order to determine the share of the market affected by the conduct of the undertaking in a dominant position, it is not possible only to take into consideration the contestable share of customers' demand.

190 In the present case, Dell's market share was 14.58% in the first quarter of 2003 and increased to 16.34% in the fourth quarter of 2005, as is apparent from recital 1580 of the contested decision. Given that, according to that decision, Intel granted rebates to Dell on condition that Dell purchase all its x86 CPU requirements from it, that means that between 2003 and 2005 Intel had already foreclosed between 14.58% and 16.34% of the market solely by the rebates granted to Dell.

191 That share of the market must be regarded as significant, in the light of the fact that competitors of the undertaking in a dominant position are entitled to benefit from competition on the merits for the entire market and not just for a part of it.

192 During 2006 and 2007, the share of the market affected was smaller, as the conduct found by the Commission in the contested decision concerned only MSH, by exclusivity payments, and Lenovo, by naked restrictions between June and December 2006 and exclusivity rebates during 2007.

193 In that regard, it should be pointed out that the Commission was right to conclude that there had been a single and continuous infringement, as will be explained in more detail in paragraphs 1561 to 1563 below. In the

case of a single and continuous infringement, it cannot be required that, during the whole of the period covered, a significant part of the market was affected by the conduct at issue. It is sufficient in that regard to carry out a global assessment of the part of the market which was foreclosed on average (see, to that effect, Case T-155/06 Tomra, paragraph 72 above, paragraph 243).

194 In the present case, the expert report that the applicant provided as an annex to the reply and which bears the reference C.1 indicates, in paragraph 48, that the share of the global market concerned by the conduct described in the contested decision was approximately 14% on average during the total period of the infringement found by the Commission, if the calculation is not limited to only the contestable share of the demand of the customers concerned. The Court is of the view that such a share must be regarded as significant.

195 With respect, next, to the applicant's argument that its supply contracts were only of short duration or that they could be terminated at 30 days' notice, it should be noted that the relevant criterion is not the duration of the notice period for terminating a contract or the fixed duration of an individual contract which forms part of a series of successive contracts, but the overall period during which the applicant applies exclusivity rebates and payments vis-à-vis a customer (see paragraphs 112 and 113 above). In the present case, that period amounted to approximately five years in the case of MSH, approximately three years in the case of Dell and NEC, more than two years in the case of HP and approximately one year in the case of Lenovo. The grant of exclusivity rebates and payments during such periods is generally capable of restricting competition. That holds especially true in relation to a market such as the CPU market, which is characterised by a high level of dynamism and short product-life cycles.

196 Lastly, with respect to the applicant's arguments concerning the lack of formal exclusivity obligations, OEMs' buying power and the relevance of the AEC test for the assessment of the exclusivity payments, reference should be made to paragraphs 106, 138 and 139 and to paragraphs 140 to 166 above respectively.

197 Accordingly, on the basis of the foregoing considerations, it is permissible to conclude that, in the contested decision, the Commission demonstrated to the requisite legal standard and according to an analysis of the circumstances of the case that the exclusivity rebates and payments

granted by the applicant to Dell, HP, NEC, Lenovo and MSH were capable of restricting competition.

3. The legal characterisation of the so-called 'naked restrictions'

198 In the contested decision, the Commission characterises as abuses three practices which it called 'naked restrictions'. According to the Commission, those three practices had a common strand, namely that the applicant granted payments to the OEMs in order that the OEMs delay, cancel or in some other way restrict the marketing of certain AMD-based products. More precisely, the grant of payments was subject to the following conditions:

- first, HP was to direct HP's AMD-based x86 CPU corporate desktops to small and medium-sized business (SMB) and Government, Educational and Medical ('GEM') customers rather than to enterprise business customers;
- second, HP was to preclude its channel partners from stocking HP's AMD-based x86 CPU corporate desktops so that such desktops would only be available to customers by ordering them from HP either directly or via HP channel partners acting as sales agent;
- third, Acer, HP and Lenovo were to delay or cancel the launch of computers equipped with AMD CPUs.

199 In order to provide a statement of reasons for characterising the naked restrictions as abusive, the Commission relied, at recitals 1643 and 1671 of the contested decision, on Case T-228/97 Irish Sugar v Commission [1999] ECR II-2969; 'Irish Sugar'. In addition, the Commission found, at recital 1643, that an infringement of Article 82 EC may also result from the object of the practices pursued by a dominant undertaking. Moreover, the Commission stated, at recitals 1670, 1672, 1678 and 1679 of the contested decision, that the naked restrictions had had an effect on the OEMs' decision-making process, since those OEMs had delayed, cancelled or in some other way restricted the marketing of their computers equipped with AMD CPUs, notwithstanding consumers' demand for those products. Lastly, at recital 1642 of the contested decision, the Commission stated that the restrictions formed part of a single strategy to foreclose AMD from the market.

200 The applicant claims, first, that the Commission is required to demonstrate that the practices are capable of restricting competition 'in economic terms'. Second, the practices at issue in the case in point differ from those that gave rise to Irish Sugar, paragraph 199 above. Third, the Commission, by censuring naked restrictions, wrongly created a new type of abuse falling within Article 82 EC.

201 First of all, it should be recalled that a foreclosure effect occurs not only where access to the market is made impossible for competitors, but also where that access is made more difficult (see paragraph 88 above).

202 In the case in point, the grant of payments subject to the three conditions set out in paragraph 198 above was capable of making access to the market more difficult for AMD. The grant of payments subject to the first of those conditions was capable of making the marketing of AMD's products more difficult, since it induced HP not to proactively sell AMD-based x86 CPU corporate desktops to a predefined group of customers. The grant of payments subject to the second of those conditions was capable of making the marketing of AMD products more difficult, given that it induced HP not to sell AMD-based x86 CPU corporate desktops via its channel partners, unless the latter acted as sales agents. Lastly, the grant of payments subject to the third of those conditions was capable of making the marketing of AMD products more difficult, because it induced HP, Lenovo and Acer to refrain from any sale of a certain type of AMD-based x86 CPU computer, at least during a certain period and, in the case of HP, in a certain region, namely the Europe, Middle-East and Africa region ('the EMEA region'). The applicant's conduct of making the grant of payments subject to those conditions was therefore capable of making the marketing of computers equipped with x86 AMD CPUs more difficult for the OEMs concerned. Given that those OEMs were customers of AMD, the conduct was at the same time capable of making access to the market more difficult for AMD, thus causing interference with the structure of competition on the x86 CPU market in which, precisely because of the applicant's position, the degree of competition was already weakened.

203 Next, it should be pointed out that, for the purposes of applying Article 82 EC, showing an anti-competitive object and an anti-competitive effect may, in some cases, be one and the same thing. If it is shown that the object pursued by the conduct of an undertaking in a dominant position is to restrict competition, that conduct will also be liable to have such

an effect (see Case T-340/03 France Télécom v Commission [2007] ECR II-107, paragraph 195 and the case-law cited).

204 That is so in the present case. The scope of the three conditions set out in paragraph 198 above was limited to AMD products, so that that undertaking must be regarded as the individual target of the applicant's practices. The only interest that an undertaking in a dominant position may have in preventing in a targeted manner the marketing of products equipped with a product of a specific competitor is to harm that competitor. Consequently, by applying naked restrictions vis-à-vis HP, Lenovo and Acer, the applicant pursued an anti-competitive object.

205 Lastly, it must be stated that an undertaking in a dominant position has a special responsibility not to impair, by conduct falling outside the scope of competition on the merits, genuine undistorted competition in the common market (see, to that effect, AstraZeneca, paragraph 64 above, paragraph 355 and the case-law cited). The grant of payments to customers in consideration of restrictions on the marketing of products equipped with a product of a specific competitor clearly falls outside the scope of competition on the merits.

206 Accordingly, it is permissible to conclude that the implementation of each of the so-called 'naked restrictions' amounted to an abuse of a dominant position within the meaning of Article 82 EC.

207 That conclusion is also confirmed by Irish Sugar, paragraph 199 above. In paragraphs 226 and 233 of that judgment, the General Court found that there was an abuse, since the dominant undertaking had agreed with one wholesaler and one retailer to swap competing retail sugar products for its own product. The Court found that the applicant in that case had undermined the competition structure which the market concerned might have acquired through the entry of a new product, by swapping the competing products on a market in which it held more than 80% of the sales volume. The reasoning underlying that judgment is also applicable to the case in point. A marketing restriction which targets a competitor's products undermines the competition structure, since it impedes in a targeted manner the placing on the market of that competitor's products.

208 The applicant's arguments cannot call that conclusion into question.

209 First, it is necessary to reject the applicant's argument that the Commission is required to demonstrate the capability of restricting

competition 'in economic terms'. In that regard, it should be observed that the applicant does not even specify what it means by 'economic terms'. Given that the three so-called 'naked restrictions' practices clearly fall outside the scope of competition on the merits (see paragraph 205 above), the Commission was not required to demonstrate their capability of restricting competition in more detail. Moreover, it should be observed that, by relying on Irish Sugar, paragraph 199 above, and the anti-competitive object of the practices, the Commission explained how they were abusive to the requisite legal standard.

210 In that regard, it is also necessary to reject the applicant's argument that the Commission was required to demonstrate the possibility or probability of foreclosure of competition, rather than refer to the anti-competitive object of the practices. Given that the anti-competitive object is indissociable in the case in point from the potential effect of the so-called 'naked restrictions' practices (see paragraphs 203 and 204 above), it must be considered that the Commission did not err in relying on their anti-competitive object.

211 Moreover, it should be noted that, in the contested decision, the Commission did not rely exclusively on the anti-competitive object of the three naked restrictions. In addition to referring to Irish Sugar, paragraph 199 above, it relied on additional circumstances confirming the capability of the naked restrictions to restrict competition, even though reference to such circumstances is not essential in order to characterise them as abusive under Article 82 EC.

212 In the first place, the Commission demonstrated to the requisite legal standard that the payments which were subject to the conditions set out in paragraph 198 above were a factor which had been taken into account by HP (see paragraphs 882 to 890 below), Lenovo (see paragraphs 1215 to 1220 below) and Acer (see paragraphs 1367 to 1369 below) in their decisions to delay, cancel or in some other way restrict the marketing of their computers equipped with AMD CPUs. That confirms the capability of those payments to restrict competition. In that context, it should be noted that characterisation of a naked restriction as abusive depends solely on the capability to restrict competition, and that characterisation does not therefore require proof of an actual effect on the market or of a causal link (see, as regards exclusivity rebates, paragraphs 103 and 104 above).

213 In the second place, the Commission established that the naked restrictions were part of a long-term comprehensive strategy to foreclose AMD from the strategically most important sales channels (see paragraphs 1523 to 1552 below).

214 Lastly, in so far as the applicant submits, in paragraphs 307 to 311 of the application, that the payments concerning the naked restriction applied vis-à-vis Lenovo obtain a positive AEC test result, it must be stated that the AEC test does not constitute an instrument which is capable of proving that a naked restriction is not of an anti-competitive nature. Even if the applicant succeeded in demonstrating that the naked restriction applied vis-à-vis Lenovo would obtain a positive AEC test result, that would not deprive that practice either of its anti-competitive object or of its capability to make access to the market more difficult for the competitor.

215 Second, it is necessary to reject the applicant's argument that the naked restrictions at issue in the contested decision differ too much from the practice censured in the case which gave rise to Irish Sugar, paragraph 199 above, for the Commission to be able to characterise them as abusive. The differences relied upon by the applicant between Irish Sugar and the present case are legally irrelevant.

216 First of all, whilst it is true that Irish Sugar, paragraph 199 above, relates to the arrival of a new product of a new undertaking on the market, the fact remains that Article 82 EC generally prohibits abusive practices capable of limiting markets, irrespective of whether new products of a new undertaking are prevented from entering the market or existing products of an established competitor are disadvantaged. In the present case, even if AMD were to be regarded as a competitor that was already established and even if the products concerned by the naked restrictions could not be characterised as new, those circumstances would not in any way alter the capability of the practices to make access to the market more difficult for AMD. Nor would those circumstances call in question the manner in which the practices concerned targeted AMD. Neither the capability of making access to the market more difficult for AMD nor the anti-competitive object of the naked restrictions depends on whether those restrictions concern a new product of a new undertaking on the market.

217 Next, in so far as the applicant claims that, in Irish Sugar, paragraph 199 above, the General Court relied on express financial threats, it must be stated that the fact that the applicant communicated to the OEMs that they

risked losing preferential rebates, in the case of HP and Acer, or that it would refuse to increase funding, in the case of Lenovo, in the event of infringement of the anti-competitive conditions set out in paragraph 198 above provides a sufficient basis on which to conclude that the applicant's announcements were capable of inducing the OEMs concerned to comply with those conditions.

218 Lastly, the applicant submits that the case which gave rise to Irish Sugar, paragraph 199 above, can be distinguished from the case in point in so far as, in the latter case, AMD was not forced to leave the market and even increased its market share. In the applicant's submission, AMD's failure to achieve greater success was due to its own limitations. However, the question whether the naked restrictions implemented by the applicant were capable of restricting competition does not depend on AMD having actually been foreclosed. In order to demonstrate that capability, proof of an actual effect on the market is not necessary (see paragraph 212 above). Moreover, it should be observed that the various marketing channels concerned by the naked restrictions were barred to AMD CPUs during the periods concerned. Furthermore, to the extent that the applicant relies on AMD's commercial success and the commercial limitations of that undertaking, its line of argument must be rejected for the reasons set out in paragraph 186 above.

219 Third, it is necessary to reject the applicant's argument that the use of the concept of 'naked restriction' constitutes a novel type of abuse. It must be stated that the legal characterisation of an abusive practice does not depend on the name given to it, but on the substantive criteria used in that regard. Thus, the mere use of the concept of 'naked restriction' does not provide a sufficient basis on which to conclude that the substantive criteria applied are new. As regards the substantive criteria applied in the present case, it is clear from the wording of point (b) of the second subparagraph of Article 82 EC that limiting markets constitutes an abuse. Moreover, it is not novel in competition law that a practice which clearly does not come within competition on the merits is regarded as unlawful (see, to that effect, Hoffmann-La Roche, paragraph 71 above, paragraph 91, and Case C-62/86 AKZO v Commission [1991] ECR I-3359, paragraph 70).

220 Lastly, even if the characterisation as abusive of the practices at issue were indeed 'novel', that would not call in question the Commission's power to prohibit them. Even in the area of the calculation of fines, the General

Court has already held that the fact that conduct with the same features has not been examined in past decisions does not exonerate an undertaking (see, to that effect, Michelin I, paragraph 74 above, paragraph 107, and AstraZeneca, paragraph 64 above, paragraph 901).

B – The Commission's jurisdiction

1. Arguments of the parties

221 The applicant, supported by ACT, points out that Articles 81 and 82 EC do not have unlimited territorial scope and that, accordingly, in order to assume jurisdiction over conduct occurring outside the European Union, the Commission must establish a direct causal connection with the territory of the European Union, by adducing strong evidence of the actual implementation of the conduct at issue leading to a substantial effect on competition within the European Union. It is also established that where trade with third countries is involved, even where implementation of the practices at issue takes place within the European Union, the Commission must also prove that its effects within the European Union are immediate, substantial, direct and foreseeable.

222 The applicant claims that, by way of example, the contested decision fails to satisfy the criteria set out in the previous paragraph by challenging Intel's agreement with Lenovo in the second half of 2006 regarding a notebook computer for the domestic Chinese market.

223 Even if the Commission's approach — according to which, as regards the rebates and naked restrictions at issue, it could establish an abuse of a dominant position without demonstrating the effects of those rebates and restrictions — were correct, the Commission is none the less required to demonstrate that they have an effect in the European Union to establish its jurisdiction. The issue of territorial jurisdiction is separate and distinct, arising from public international law.

224 During the written procedure, the applicant claimed that, in relation to all the agreements involving entities located outside the European Union, namely Dell, HP, NEC, Acer, and Lenovo, the contested decision fails to establish that the Commission has jurisdiction.

225 At the hearing, the applicant stated that it was limiting that plea solely to the conduct vis-à-vis Acer and Lenovo, formal note of which was taken in the minutes of the hearing.

226 In relation to Acer and Lenovo, the applicant stated that their manufacturing facilities were outside the EEA, and that they did not purchase CPUs in the EEA from Intel or AMD. The conduct at issue concerned sales of CPUs to customers in Asia, namely in Taiwan as regards Acer and in China as regards Lenovo, and that conduct was implemented in Asia. The fact that a certain number of Acer and Lenovo computers might subsequently have been sold within the EEA is irrelevant to the question of the implementation of the conduct complained of.

227 Given that Intel's conduct in relation to Acer and Lenovo concerned sales of CPUs in Asia, the immediate effects of that conduct were felt in Asia and not in the EEA. Sales of computers, which constitute the only conduct that might have concerned the EEA, were carried out by third parties, namely Acer and Lenovo, which were not controlled by Intel.

228 The volume of computers concerned was very small and the effect in the EEA cannot be regarded as substantial.

229 At the hearing, the applicant also claimed that the conduct at issue was not capable of affecting trade between Member States.

230 The Commission contests the arguments of the applicant and of ACT.

2. Findings of the Court

a) Preliminary observations

231 First of all, it should be noted that, in the case-law of the Court of Justice and the General Court, two approaches have been followed in order to establish that the Commission's jurisdiction is justified under the rules of public international law.

232 The first approach is based on the principle of territoriality. That approach was followed in Joined Cases 89/85, 104/85, 114/85, 116/85, 117/85 and 125/85 to 129/85 Ahlström Osakeyhtiö and Others v Commission [1988] ECR 5193, 'Woodpulp'). In paragraph 16 of that judgment, the Court held that it was necessary to distinguish two elements of conduct, namely the formation of the agreement, decision or concerted practice and the implementation thereof. If the applicability of prohibitions laid down under competition law were made to depend on the place where the agreement, decision or concerted practice was formed, the result would obviously be to give undertakings an easy means of evading those

prohibitions. The Court therefore held that the decisive factor is the place where it is implemented.

233 The second approach is based on the qualified effects of the practices in the European Union. That approach was followed in Case T-102/96 Gencor v Commission [1999] ECR II-753, 'Gencor'. In paragraph 90 of that judgment, the Court held that application of Council Regulation (EEC) No 4064/89 of 21 December 1989 on the control of concentrations between undertakings (OJ 1989 L 395, p. 1), as corrected (OJ 1990 L 257, p. 13), is justified under public international law when it is foreseeable that a proposed concentration will have an immediate and substantial effect in the European Union.

234 By submitting that where trade with third countries is involved, even where implementation of the practices at issue takes place within the European Union, the Commission must also prove the existence of immediate, substantial, direct and foreseeable effects within the European Union, the applicant's reasoning amounts to an assertion that implementation and qualified effects in the European Union are cumulative conditions.

235 The Commission stated, at the hearing, that, in the present case, its jurisdiction was justified, first, under the doctrine of implementation of the practices at issue in the EEA, which was followed in Woodpulp, paragraph 232 above, and, second, under the effects doctrine, which was followed in Gencor, paragraph 233 above.

236 In that regard, the Court would point out that demonstrating the implementation of the practices at issue in the EEA or demonstrating qualified effects are alternative and not cumulative approaches for the purposes of establishing that the Commission's jurisdiction is justified under the rules of public international law.

237 In Woodpulp, paragraph 232 above, the Court of Justice relied solely on the implementation of the conduct at issue in the territory of the European Union.

238 The applicant may not rely on the fact that Advocate General Darmon stated, in point 82 of his Opinion in Woodpulp, paragraph 232 above, that it would be for the Court 'to ascertain whether the effects of the conduct alleged by the Commission were substantial, direct and foreseeable in order to determine whether the Commission was right in exercising jurisdiction

over the applicants'. The Advocate General proposed that the Court should rely on the effects of the conduct at issue in the territory of the European Union in order to establish the Commission's jurisdiction. The Court did not follow the Advocate General's proposal and relied on the implementation of the agreement in the European Union. It therefore follows from the judgment of the Court in that case that, where the Commission's jurisdiction can be established on the basis of the implementation of the conduct at issue in the European Union, it is not necessary to examine whether there were any effects in order to establish the Commission's jurisdiction.

239 The applicant relies in that context also on Gencor, paragraph 233 above.

240 However, in Gencor, paragraph 233 above (paragraphs 89 to 101), the General Court relied solely on the qualified effects in order to establish that the Commission's jurisdiction was justified under the rules of public international law.

241 It is indeed true that, in paragraph 87 of that judgment, the Court observed that, according to Woodpulp, paragraph 232 above, the criterion as to the implementation of an agreement is satisfied by mere sale within the European Union. However, paragraph 87 forms part of the reasoning of the Court by which the latter held that Regulation No 4064/89 did not, for the purpose of defining its territorial scope, ascribe greater importance to production operations than to sales operations (Gencor, paragraph 233 above, paragraphs 85 to 88). In that context, the Court rejected an argument of the applicant based on Woodpulp, paragraph 232 above, by holding that, according to that judgment, the criterion as to the implementation of an agreement is satisfied by mere sales. The Court therefore rejected the applicant's argument that it follows from Woodpulp, paragraph 232 above, that greater importance is ascribed to production activities than to sales activities.

242 Next, the Court examined, in paragraphs 89 to 101 of Gencor, paragraph 233 above, whether the application of Regulation No 4064/89 in that case was consistent with public international law. In that context, the Court confined itself to examining whether the criteria of immediate, substantial and foreseeable effect were satisfied.

243 It therefore follows from Gencor, paragraph 233 above, that, in order to justify the Commission's jurisdiction according to the rules of public

international law, it is sufficient that the criteria of immediate, substantial and foreseeable effect in the European Union be satisfied.

244 It follows from the foregoing that, in order to justify the Commission's jurisdiction under public international law, it is sufficient to establish either the qualified effects of the practice in the European Union or that it was implemented in the European Union.

245 In another connection, it should be noted that, in the contested decision, the Commission does not deal expressly with the question whether the Commission's jurisdiction is justified under the rules of public international law. In that regard, the Commission states that it dealt, at recitals 1749 to 1753 of the contested decision, with the question whether trade was affected between Member States.

246 Furthermore, the Commission states, without being contradicted on that point by the applicant, that, during the administrative procedure, the applicant never questioned the Commission's international jurisdiction.

247 In that context, the Court notes that the wording of Article 82 EC contains two elements which relate to a link with the territory of the European Union. First, Article 82 EC requires the existence of a dominant position 'within the common market or in a substantial part of it'. Second, it requires that trade between Member States be capable of being affected by the conduct in question. In the contested decision, the Commission established the existence of a dominant position by the applicant at a worldwide level, which includes the common market. Moreover, at recitals 1749 to 1753 of that decision, it expressly examined the effect on trade between Member States.

248 It is true that the question whether the Commission's jurisdiction is justified under public international law is a question separate from that of the criteria laid down by Article 82 EC. In that regard, it should be observed that the criterion of the effect on trade between Member States is intended to define the sphere of application of Community rules in relation to national laws (see, to that effect, Joined Cases 6/73 and 7/73 Istituto Chemioterapico Italiano and Commercial Solvents v Commission [1974] ECR 223, paragraph 31).

249 None the less, in the light of the fact, first, that the Commission took a view in the contested decision on the two criteria laid down in Article 82 EC concerning a link with the territory of the European Union and, second,

that the applicant did not question, during the administrative procedure, the Commission's international jurisdiction, it was not essential for the Commission to provide an express statement of reasons in the contested decision regarding that question (see also, as regards the obligation to provide a statement of reasons for the Commission's jurisdiction, Case 48/69 Imperial Chemical Industries v Commission [1972] ECR 619, paragraphs 143 to 145). The applicant moreover specified, at the hearing, that its plea did not concern a failure to state reasons, formal note of which was taken in the minutes of the hearing.

b) Qualified effects

1) Preliminary observations

250 The applicant claims that the Commission's failure to examine the existence of substantial, direct and foreseeable effects in the European Union is a particularly significant failing in circumstances where the Commission states, at recital 1685 of the contested decision, that it does not need 'to prove the actual effects of an abuse under Article 82 [EC]'.

251 In that regard, the Court would point out that the Commission is not obliged to establish the existence of actual effects in order to justify its jurisdiction under public international law. The criteria of immediate, substantial and foreseeable effects do not mean that the effect must also be actual. It is for the Commission to ensure that competition within the common market is protected against threats to the effective functioning thereof.

252 Accordingly, the view cannot be taken that the Commission is required to confine itself to pursuing and punishing abuse which achieved the intended result and in respect of which the threat to the functioning of competition materialised. The Commission cannot be expected to adopt a passive position where there is a threat to the effective competition structure in the common market and may therefore intervene also in cases in which the threat did not materialise or has not yet materialised.

253 In addition, in the present case, the conduct vis-à-vis Acer and Lenovo was intended to produce effects within the common market.

254 The conduct vis-à-vis Acer consisted in granting payments conditional upon Acer's delaying the launch of an AMD-based notebook worldwide. Such a financial incentive was intended to ensure that, during a given

period, a certain Acer computer model would not be available on the market anywhere in the world, including in the EEA.

255 The conduct vis-à-vis Lenovo consisted, first, in granting payments to Lenovo conditional upon Lenovo's delaying and finally cancelling the launch of its AMD-based x86 CPU notebooks. That conduct was therefore intended to ensure that AMD-based computer models of Lenovo would not be available anywhere in the world, including in the EEA. Second, the conduct vis-à-vis Lenovo consisted in granting rebates at a level that was conditional upon Lenovo obtaining all of its notebook x86 CPU supplies from Intel. That conduct was intended to ensure that no Lenovo AMD-based notebook would be available on the market, including in the EEA. Intel's conduct was therefore intended to produce effects also in the EEA. Under these circumstances, the question whether the applicant achieved the intended result is irrelevant in the context of the examination of whether the Commission's jurisdiction is justified under public international law.

256 Moreover, the Court observes that the applicant itself relies on Case T-204/03 Haladjian Frères v Commission [2006] ECR II-3779, and in particular on paragraph 167 thereof, in which the Court stated:

'[I]n order to justify the application of the competition rules to an agreement concerning products purchased in the United States for sale in the Community, that agreement must, on the basis of a range of elements of fact and of law, make it possible to envisage with a sufficient degree of probability that it is capable of having a more than insignificant influence on competition in the Community and on trade between Member States (see, to that effect, [Case C-306/96] Javico [1998] ECR I-1983], paragraphs 16 and 18). The mere fact that conduct produces certain effects, no matter what they may be, on the Community economy does not in itself constitute a sufficiently close link to be able to found Community competence. In order to be capable of being taken into account, that effect must be substantial, that is to say, appreciable and not negligible.'

257 That judgment does not therefore require the existence of actual effects on competition in the European Union, but only that it be sufficiently probable that the agreement at issue is capable of having a more than insignificant influence there. In that regard, it should be noted that that finding did not relate expressly to the question whether the Commission's jurisdiction was justified under public international law, but that it was made in the context of the examination of the question whether the criteria

laid down in Article 81 EC were fulfilled. None the less, that judgment, which is relied on by the applicant, is an element confirming that the effects of conduct on competition do not necessarily have to be actual in order to constitute a sufficiently close link with the European Union capable of founding the Commission's jurisdiction.

258 It is therefore necessary to examine whether the three criteria of substantial, immediate and foreseeable effect are satisfied in the case in point.

2) **Acer**

2.1) Substantial effect

259 The applicant points out that the delay to which the Commission refers in the Decision concerned an AMD-based 64-bit technology notebook model. The applicant states that, in the fourth quarter of 2003, only 100 000 CPUs of that type were available worldwide. In the applicant's submission, Acer might have purchased at most approximately 4 000 units of that type, and most of Acer's computers concerned by the delayed launch would in any event have been sold outside the EEA. The effects in the EEA could not therefore in any case have been substantial.

260 The Commission challenges the figure of 4 000 units. However, it admitted at the hearing that the quantity of computers concerned was modest. It none the less stated at the hearing that, given that there was an overall strategy aimed at foreclosing Intel's sole important competitor and that there was a single and continuous infringement, it was not appropriate to view the effects of the various instances of conduct in isolation.

261 As regards the substantial nature of the effects, the Court would point out, first of all, that it is not necessary that the European Union or the EEA be more affected than other regions of the world (see, to that effect, Gencor, paragraph 233 above, paragraph 98).

262 Moreover, the EEA constitutes a significant part of the world market. By way of illustration, it should be noted that, according to recital 1775 of the contested decision, sales of computers incorporating Intel x86 CPUs in the EMEA region amounted to approximately 32% of world sales. Furthermore, the Commission found that the value of Intel's sales to undertakings established in the EEA amounted to approximately 80% of sales in the EMEA region.

263 It should also be noted that it is clear from the evidence cited in the contested decision, in particular from the email cited in paragraph 1240 below, that Acer had planned to sell in Europe the model concerned by the delayed launch. It is therefore necessary to reject the applicant's argument put forward at the hearing that it is possible that the computers in question would have all been sold outside the EEA.

264 The grant of a financial incentive, for the purpose of encouraging a customer to delay at a worldwide level the launch of a computer incorporating a competitor's CPU sales of which were planned in Europe, is capable of having at least potential effects in the EEA.

265 ACT maintained that it was apparent from the email cited in paragraph 1240 below that the naked restriction alleged by the Commission concerned only limitations on Acer's sales to countries outside of Europe.

266 In that regard, it is sufficient to note that, in the end, Acer committed to delaying the launch of the computer in question at a worldwide level (see paragraphs 1246, 1247, 1268 and 1269 below). ACT's argument that the Commission found an infringement that concerned only sales of Acer to countries outside of Europe therefore has no factual basis.

267 Moreover, it should be pointed out that the Commission was right in finding that the various instances of conduct described in the contested decision were part of a single and continuous infringement (see paragraphs 1561 to 1563 below).

268 In order to examine whether the effects are substantial, the various instances of conduct forming part of a single and continuous infringement must not be considered in isolation. It is on the contrary sufficient that the single infringement as a whole be capable of having substantial effects.

269 As regards the effect on trade between Member States within the meaning of Article 82 EC, it is clear from the case-law that it is necessary to take into consideration the consequences of an abuse of a dominant position for the effective competition structure in the common market (see Case 22/79 Greenwich Film Production [1979] ECR 3275, paragraph 11 and the case-law cited). The Court of Justice has also made clear that, in considering whether Article 82 EC is applicable, the performance of certain contracts cannot be assessed in isolation but must be viewed in the light of the activities of the undertaking in question as a whole (see, to that effect, Greenwich Film Production, paragraph 12). As regards the criterion of the

effect on trade between Member States, the Court has therefore expressly held that certain contracts must not be considered in an isolated manner.

270 The same conclusion applies, in the case of a single and continuous infringement, when considering whether the Commission's jurisdiction is justified under public international law. Undertakings cannot be allowed to escape application of the competition rules by combining several practices pursuing the same objective, when each practice viewed in isolation is not liable to produce a substantial effect in the European Union but the practices, taken together, are liable to produce such an effect.

271 In the present case, it should be recalled that the single and continuous infringement, viewed as a whole, affected on average, according to the calculations by the applicant's adviser, approximately 14% of the global market if those calculations are not limited to only the contestable share; this must be regarded as a significant share of the market (see paragraph 194 above).

272 That is sufficient to establish that the potential effects of the applicant's practices were substantial.

273 Moreover, the Court finds that the Commission demonstrated to the requisite legal standard that the applicant had pursued a long-term comprehensive strategy to foreclose AMD from the strategically most important sales channels (see paragraphs 1523 to 1552 below).

274 It is apparent from the case-law that, in relation to the criterion of the effect on trade between Member States, it is necessary to take into consideration the repercussions for the effective competition structure in the common market resulting from the elimination of a competitor (see, to that effect, Istituto Chemioterapico Italiano and Commercial Solvents v Commission, paragraph 248 above, paragraph 33, and Joined Cases T-24/93 to T-26/93 and T-28/93 Compagnie maritime belge transports and Others v Commission [1996] ECR II-1201, paragraph 203). Changes to the structure of the market must also be taken into consideration when it comes to determining whether there are substantial effects within the EEA in the context of the examination of the question whether the Commission's jurisdiction is justified under public international law (see, to that effect, Gencor, paragraph 233 above, paragraphs 94 and 96).

275 In that respect, the Court would point out that not only is the elimination of a competitor capable of having repercussions for the

competition structure in the common market, but that conduct capable of weakening the applicant's sole significant competitor at the worldwide level, by foreclosing it from the most important sales channels, such as the conduct at issue in the present case, is also capable of having repercussions for the effective competition structure in the common market. Accordingly, the finding that the potential effects of the applicant's conduct must be regarded as substantial is also justified on account of the potential effects on the effective competition structure in the common market.

276 It follows from the foregoing that the potential effects of the applicant's conduct must be regarded as substantial.

2.2) **Immediate effect**

277 Intel's conduct was intended to produce an immediate effect in the EEA and was capable of doing so.

278 That conduct was intended to induce Acer and was capable of inducing it to delay the launch of an AMD-based notebook worldwide, including in the EEA. The delay in the launch means that, during a certain period, a certain AMD-based computer model is not available, including in the EEA. It is a direct effect and not merely a knock-on effect.

279 Contrary to the submissions of the applicant and ACT, the fact that Intel did not sell CPUs to Acer in the EEA does not mean that the effect in the EEA of Intel's conduct could only have been indirect. The condition to which those payments were subject, namely the postponement of the launch of a certain computer model worldwide, including in the EEA, concerned directly sales of computers by Acer.

280 Moreover, the single and continuous infringement committed by the applicant, viewed as a whole, was capable of having the immediate effect of weakening the applicant's sole significant competitor by foreclosing it from the most important sales channels and therefore of changing the effective competition structure in the common market.

2.3) **Foreseeable effect**

281 The effect that a certain AMD-based computer model would not be available during the postponement period, including in the EEA, was foreseeable for the applicant. Indeed, that was the intended effect of its conduct.

282 Similarly, the weakening of the applicant's sole significant competitor was foreseeable for it and intended by it.

3) Lenovo

3.1) The naked restrictions

i) The postponement of the launch concerning the Chinese market

283 The applicant claims that the first postponement of the launch alleged by the Commission in the contested decision relates to the delayed launch of two AMD-based notebook models in China (see in that regard paragraphs 1035 and 1037 below). In the applicant's submission, that agreement only affected the Chinese market and was not implemented in the European Union.

284 In that regard, it is sufficient to note that, in the contested decision, the Commission does not make a finding of a breach of Article 82 EC in respect of the postponement of the launch of AMD-based notebooks in China (see paragraph 1042 below). The applicant's line of argument regarding the Commission's lack of jurisdiction to punish that conduct is therefore ineffective.

ii) The postponement of the launch concerning the worldwide market

285 The postponement of the launch at issue in the contested decision concerns the delayed launch of those computer models at the worldwide level. In that regard, the applicant stated, at the hearing, that it was apparent from Annex A.120 to the application that, for the two computer models concerned by the postponed launch, the planned level of sales was very low.

286 In that regard, it should be noted that it is apparent from that annex that, on 1 June 2006, the projected sales figures in the EMEA region in respect of the fourth quarter of 2006 for the two notebook models concerned by the postponement of the launch were 5 400 and 4 250 units.

287 At the hearing, the applicant suggested that it was possible that all those computers were intended for areas of the EMEA region outside the EEA.

288 In that regard, the Court observes that this suggestion is mere speculation by the applicant in support of which it has not put forward any argument. It is true that the exact volume of the planned sales in the EEA is not apparent from Annex A.120 to the application. It should however be pointed out that the EEA is a very important part of the EMEA region.

289 It is clearly apparent from Annex A.120 to the application that Lenovo had planned sales in the EMEA region. That is sufficient for a finding that there were at least potential effects in the EEA, in the absence of any specific indicia which might suggest that all the planned sales concerned parts of the EMEA region outside the EEA.

290 It is true that the number of units concerned in the EMEA region was modest. However, the Court would point out that the conduct vis-à-vis Lenovo formed part of a single and continuous infringement and that it is sufficient that that infringement, viewed as a whole, was capable of having substantial effects, which is the situation in the present case (see paragraphs 267 to 276 above).

291 As regards the immediate nature of the effect and of its foreseeability, the points set out in paragraphs 277 to 282 above apply mutatis mutandis.

3.2) The exclusivity rebates

292 According to the contested decision, Intel granted rebates to Lenovo between January 2007 and December 2007 at a level that was conditional on Lenovo's obtaining all of its notebook x86 CPU supplies from Intel.

293 The contested decision thus refers to a financial incentive granted by Intel to Lenovo in order to encourage it to use exclusively x86 CPUs produced by Intel in its notebooks. That conduct was capable of having the immediate effect that no Lenovo notebook incorporating an x86 CPU of a competitor of Intel was available anywhere in the world, including in the EEA. The fact that Intel sells CPUs, whilst Lenovo sells computers, does not mean that the effect can be only indirect. If Lenovo obtains all its notebook x86 CPU requirements from Intel, that means directly and necessarily that it cannot manufacture or sell any notebook incorporating an x86 CPU of a competitor.

294 That effect was foreseeable for Intel and even intended by it.

295 As regards the substantial nature of the effect, it is sufficient to point out that the exclusivity rebates formed part of a single and continuous

infringement which, viewed as a whole, was capable of having substantial effects in the territory of the European Union and the EEA, which is sufficient (see paragraphs 267 to 276 above). It is not therefore necessary to examine whether the exclusivity rebates granted to Lenovo, viewed in isolation, were capable of having a substantial effect in that territory.

296 It follows from the foregoing that the conduct of Intel to which the Commission refers in the contested decision was capable of having a substantial, immediate and foreseeable effect within the EEA. Accordingly, the Commission's jurisdiction to punish that conduct is justified under the rules of public international law.

297 It is therefore for the sake of completeness that the implementation of the conduct at issue in the territory of the EEA will be examined below.

c) Implementation

298 The applicant claims that, according to case-law, direct sales into the European Union by the undertaking itself of the products covered by the conduct concerned are required to establish the Commission's jurisdiction. In the present case, the Commission has not established that each of the alleged acts of abuse encompassed direct sales of the relevant product, namely x86 CPUs, by Intel to purchasers in the European Union or the EEA.

299 The applicant states that it did not sell x86 CPUs to Acer or Lenovo in the EEA. Acer and Lenovo did not sell the products concerned by the contested decision, namely x86 CPUs, but computers incorporating x86 CPUs.

300 The Commission disputes the applicant's arguments.

1) Acer

301 It should be borne in mind that the implementation of the practices at issue in the European Union is sufficient to justify the Commission's jurisdiction under public international law (see, to that effect, Woodpulp, paragraph 232 above, paragraph 16).

302 It is true that, in the case which gave rise to Woodpulp, paragraph 232 above, the Court of Justice found that the agreement in question had been implemented in the common market by means of direct sales, at prices which were actually coordinated, by the participants in the agreement to

purchasers established in the European Union (paragraphs 12, 13, 16 and 17 of that judgment).

303 However, it does not follow from this that direct sales by addressees of the Commission's contested decision are the only means of implementing a practice in the European Union. The mere fact that the applicant did not sell CPUs to subsidiaries of Acer and Lenovo located in the EEA does not therefore preclude implementation of the practices at issue in the EEA.

304 In the present case, the Commission did not refer, in the contested decision, to action initiated by the applicant itself in the territory of the EEA in order to implement the naked restriction concerning Acer.

305 Nevertheless, the abuse of a dominant position consisted in the present case in the grant of a financial incentive in order to encourage Acer to postpone the launch of a certain notebook worldwide. The condition to which the payments granted by Intel were subject, namely the postponement of a certain AMD-based notebook, was therefore intended to be implemented worldwide by Acer, including in the EEA.

306 In such circumstances, it would be artificial merely to take into consideration the implementation of the practices at issue by the undertaking in a dominant position itself. On the contrary, it is also necessary to take into consideration the implementation of those practices by the customer of that undertaking.

307 In that context, the fact that the customer of the undertaking in a dominant position refrains from selling a certain computer model in the EEA for a certain period must be regarded as implementation of the naked restriction.

308 Moreover, it is apparent from the evidence cited in the contested decision that Acer took action in the EMEA region to postpone the launch of the computer at issue. It is apparent from the email cited in paragraph 1247 below, which was relied on in that respect by the Commission at the hearing, that the [confidential] at Acer was instructed to 'drop' the AMD CPU concerned for 2003, and that he would give effect to that instruction in the EMEA region.

309 It follows from the foregoing that the Commission's jurisdiction was justified also on account of the implementation of the infringement in the territory of the European Union and the EEA.

2) Lenovo

310 As regards the naked restrictions, namely the rebates granted on condition that Lenovo postpone the launch of two computer models, it should be noted that they were intended to be implemented worldwide by Lenovo, including in the EEA. It follows that the Commission's jurisdiction was justified also on account of the implementation of the infringement in that territory. In that regard, the points made in paragraphs 304 to 307 above apply mutatis mutandis.

311 As regards the exclusivity rebates, the consideration for those rebates, namely Lenovo's sole sourcing from Intel for its notebook x86 CPUs, was intended to be implemented worldwide by Lenovo, including in the EEA, by Lenovo's selling exclusively notebooks incorporating Intel x86 CPUs. In that context, the Court would point out that the intended use of the CPUs, namely their use by Lenovo in notebooks, formed part of the consideration as that consideration had been defined. Accordingly, the applicant cannot usefully rely on the argument that the market at issue concerned x86 CPUs whereas Lenovo did not sell CPUs, but computers incorporating CPUs. The consideration as defined established a direct link with the computers which would be produced and sold by Lenovo.

312 The applicant's conduct was intended to ensure that the consideration provided by Lenovo would be implemented everywhere that Lenovo sold notebooks, including in the EEA.

313 Given that the consideration as defined concerned specifically CPUs intended to be used for a certain type of product, namely notebooks, the applicant cannot properly claim that Intel had no influence on the use made by Lenovo of the Intel CPUs. Moreover, the applicant has not claimed that it was not aware that Lenovo was present in the common market and sold notebooks in that market.

314 It follows from the foregoing that, concerning the applicant's conduct vis-à-vis Lenovo, the Commission's jurisdiction is also justified on account of the implementation of the infringement in the territory of the European Union and the EEA.

d) The effect on trade between Member States

315 At the hearing, the applicant also claimed that the conduct at issue was not capable of affecting trade between Member States.

316 As regards the criterion of the effect on trade between Member States, the Commission found, at recital 1750 of the contested decision, that abuses that have an impact on the competitive structure in more than one Member State are by their very nature capable of affecting trade between Member States.

317 According to case-law, if an agreement, decision or practice is to be capable of affecting trade between Member States, it must be possible to foresee with a sufficient degree of probability, on the basis of a set of facts and points of law, that they may have an influence, direct or indirect, actual or potential, on the pattern of trade between Member States in such a way as to cause concern that they might hinder the attainment of a single market between Member States. Moreover, that effect must not be insignificant (see Javico, paragraph 256 above, paragraph 16 and the case-law cited).

318 In the present case, the applicant has not claimed that its conduct vis-à-vis Acer and Lenovo concerned only the territory of a single Member State. In disputing that trade between Member States was affected, the applicant relied rather on the fact that the effects were felt outside the EEA and that, in any event, the volume of computers concerned would have been very small, so that the effects could not in any case have been significant.

319 Nevertheless, as was observed in paragraph 269 above, it is not appropriate to consider the effects of the applicant's conduct vis-à-vis Acer and Lenovo in isolation. Viewed as a whole, the single infringement committed by the applicant was capable of having a substantial effect in the European Union and the EEA.

320 The Court must therefore reject the applicant's line of argument disputing that trade between Member States was affected.

321 It follows from all the foregoing that the applicant's line of argument challenging the Commission's jurisdiction must be rejected.

C – Procedural irregularities

[omitted]

D – Errors of assessment concerning the practices relating to the various OEMs and MSH

[omitted]

E – The evidence of an overall strategy aimed at foreclosing AMD's access to the most important sales channels

1523 According to the contested decision, the applicant implemented a long-term comprehensive strategy to foreclose AMD from the strategically most important sales channels. In that decision, the Commission based the existence of that strategy, in essence, on the following:

- the practices at issue in that decision took place during a consistent period between 2002 and 2007 (see recitals 1740 and 1745);
- the practices were carried out in the context of a growing competitive threat from AMD (see recitals 1741 and 149 to 164);
- the practices had a common strand since they were all aimed at or had the effect of foreclosing AMD from the market (see recital 1745);
- the practices allegedly concerned not only a significant number of OEMs worldwide, but also the strategically most important sales channels (see recitals 1745 and 1747)
- the practices complemented each another (see recital 1747);
- two emails dated November 1998 and sent by the [confidential] of the applicant and by its [confidential] (see recital 1747 in conjunction with footnote 2065 [footnote 2056 of the public version]);
- the applicant attempted to conceal the anti-competitive nature of its practices (see recitals 1742 and 1743).

1524 The applicant contests the existence of a comprehensive strategy. This finding is erroneous, as the infringements found regarding the individual OEMs and MSH are fragmented in relation to both products covered and time period, precluding a claim that there was a 'single' 'comprehensive strategy'. The Commission's position is incompatible with Professor P3's observations, who refuted the existence of a strategy by referring to 'contra-indicators', and in particular the growth in purchases from AMD by the OEMs concerned. The Commission does not provide any evidence of a consistent or coherent plan. The emails from 1998 do not provide any evidence of the existence of a coherent plan to foreclose AMD. Lastly, the applicant contests that it concealed the anti-competitive nature of its practices.

1525 As a preliminary point, it should be noted that proof of the existence of an overall strategy does not necessarily require direct evidence demonstrating the existence of a coherent anti-competitive plan. The Commission may rather demonstrate the existence of such a plan also by a body of evidence.

1526 As regards, next, the evidence on which the Commission relied in the contested decision, the Court notes the following.

1527 First, in so far as the applicant alleges that the practices at issue are of a fragmented nature, it must be stated that the evidence on which the Commission relied in the contested decision establishes the coherence of those practices to the requisite legal standard.

1528 In the first place, the Commission was entitled to rely on the fact that the infringements were consistent over time. The contested decision states in that regard that the practices at issue were concentrated between 2002 and 2005 and that, during the period between September 2003 and January 2004, six individual abuses occurred, namely conditional rebates or payments vis-à-vis Dell, HP, NEC and MSH, and naked restrictions vis-à-vis HP and Acer. Whilst it is true that, for a part of 2006, the contested decision finds only one illegal practice vis-à-vis MSH and for the remainder of 2006 and for 2007 only illegal practices vis-à-vis MSH and Lenovo, that weakening of the overall intensity of the applicant's anti-competitive conduct towards the end of the total period at issue does not call in question the continuity over time between the respective practices. It follows that the applicant's argument that those practices were of a fragmented nature as regards the period in question must be rejected.

1529 In the second place, the Commission correctly relied on the comparable nature and complementarity of the practices at issue in the contested decision. By contrast, the applicant's argument that the fragmented nature of the infringements stems from the differences between the products concerned is unconvincing.

1530 On the one hand, all the practices at issue in the contested decision have a common strand, since they were all capable of foreclosing AMD from the worldwide market for x86 CPUs. Thus, those practices were interconnected, given that they all concerned the same market and the same competitor of the applicant.

1531 Admittedly, the applicant claims that its practices vis-à-vis MSH can be distinguished from its practices vis-à-vis the OEMs, since they concern a retailer of electronic products that does not buy any CPUs from Intel directly and does not receive true rebates from Intel, but only marketing contributions. Moreover, the applicant complains that the Commission has failed to define a relevant product and geographic market in respect of the MSH allegations.

1532 However, the Court finds that those arguments cannot succeed in depriving the practices of the applicant at issue in the contested decision of their comparable nature and of their complementarity.

1533 In that regard, it should be recalled that the applicant's practices vis-à-vis the OEMs and MSH are, in principle, comparable, the only difference being that the exclusivity payment granted to MSH was not designed to prevent the supply of a direct customer of the applicant by a competitor, but rather the sale of competing products by a retailer further down the supply chain. The Court observes that the Commission was not required to define a separate product market or a separate geographic market as regards MSH. The applicant's practices vis-à-vis MSH were capable of restricting competition on the worldwide market for x86 CPUs. By depriving OEMs of a distribution channel for AMD-based computers, those practices were capable of having repercussions for OEMs' demand for AMD CPUs on the worldwide market for x86 CPUs. Thus, those practices tended to make it more difficult for AMD to gain access to that market (see paragraph 169 above). That market therefore constitutes at least one of the markets concerned by the applicant's conduct vis-à-vis MSH. The fact that the applicant's practice vis-à-vis MSH might also have concerned the market on which MSH operated does not undermine that conclusion. Consequently, it is not necessary to adjudicate on the question whether the market on which MSH operated was defined correctly.

1534 On the other hand, the anti-competitive mechanisms of the practices at issue in the contested decision are complementary. With respect (i) to the complementarity between (a) the exclusivity rebates and payments and (b) the naked restrictions, the Commission correctly states, at recital 1642 of the contested decision, that the scope of those restrictions is more specific than that of the exclusivity rebates and payments. The naked restrictions are shorter in duration and are focused on a specific product or line of products or specific sales channels, whereas the exclusivity agreements are longer in duration and cover at least entire business segments. Thus, within that single strategy, naked restrictions constitute tactical moves to foreclose AMD from well-identified specific products or sales channels, while exclusivity rebates and payments constitute more strategic devices to foreclose AMD from entire segments of OEMs' demand.

1535 With respect (ii) to the complementarity between (a) the exclusivity rebates granted to the OEMs and (b) the exclusivity payments vis-à-vis MSH, the Commission correctly found, at recital 1597 of the contested decision, that those practices were applied to two levels of the distribution chain. Even on the assumption, as the applicant submits, that MSH purchased only a small part of its computers from the OEMs to which the applicant granted exclusivity rebates, that would not call in question the complementarity between (a) the exclusivity rebates granted to the OEMs and (b) the exclusivity payments granted to MSH. By giving MSH an incentive to sell exclusively Intel-based computers, the applicant implemented an additional anti-competitive device which was capable of restricting also the commercial freedom of the OEMs to which it did not grant exclusivity rebates, by depriving them of a sales channel for their AMD-based computers. Thus, the applicant created an additional barrier for AMD's access to the market which was complementary to that created by the exclusivity rebates.

1536 Second, the applicant relies, on the one hand, on the fact that the infringements covered only a limited share of the market as a contra-indicator of the strategic nature of its conduct. At the hearing, the applicant stated in that regard that, for a part of 2006, the contested decision finds only one illegal practice vis-à-vis MSH and, for the remainder of 2006 and for 2007, the existence of illegal practices only vis-à-vis MSH and Lenovo (see paragraph 1528 above). The applicant added that that decision does not find that Lenovo had strategic importance comparable to Dell's and HP's. Sales of notebooks in the European Union which were potentially affected by its practices vis-à-vis Lenovo were negligible. That is also the case in respect of sales of computers potentially affected by its practices vis-à-vis MSH if those sales are considered in relation to worldwide sales. On the other hand, the applicant relies on the fact that the OEMs concerned increased their purchases from AMD during the period at issue and that that increase was greater than the growth in AMD's sales to the remainder of the market as another contra-indicator of the strategic nature of its conduct.

1537 However, on the one hand, in so far as the applicant claims that the infringements covered only a limited share of the market, it should be noted that a practice may be considered strategic even if it covers only a limited share of the market. In the present case, the strategic nature of the applicant's conduct stems from the fact that it attempted to foreclose AMD from the most important sales channels, namely Dell for the period between December 2002 and December 2005 and HP for the period between November 2002 and May 2005 (see paragraph 182 above). Moreover, with respect to 2006 and 2007, the Court finds that the coherence between the individual infringements of which the overall strategy was composed is not interrupted by the fact that the infringements concerning Lenovo and MSH were less significant than the infringements concerning Dell and HP. That conclusion applies a fortiori given that MSH was particularly strategically important so far as concerned the retail of consumer computers equipped with x86 CPUs in Europe (see paragraphs 183 and 1507 to 1511 above). In any event, it should be recalled that the foreclosed part of the market was on average significant (see paragraphs 187 to 194 above).

1538 On the other hand, in so far as the applicant relies on the increase in OEMs' purchases from AMD during the period at issue, it must be stated that that circumstance cannot even demonstrate that the applicant's practices had no effect. In the absence of the applicant's practices, it may legitimately be considered that the increase in OEMs' purchases from AMD might have been greater (see paragraph 186 above).

1539 Third, contrary to the applicant's claim, the two emails from November 1998 also provide evidence of the strategic manner in which the applicant implemented its practices. On 27 November 1998, the [confidential] of Intel wrote as follows: '[T]here is really no question that in the long run, I would like AMD output spread round the world as a low cost/low value, unbranded brand. The backstreets of Beijing are wonderful.' Similarly, on 20 November 1998, the [confidential] of Intel, wrote: 'Acknowledging that we have to face competition I think it would be better to have them selling their product with limited penetration around the world rather than high penetration in the most visible and trend setting market'. Although it is true that, in themselves, such statements could be regarded as business language which is admittedly aggressive but not suspicious, the fact remains that, in the light of the other evidence mentioned above, the two emails confirm that Intel's aim was to limit AMD's access to the market. Moreover, contrary to the applicant's claim, the mere fact that the two emails are from 1998 and therefore approximately four years before the period at issue in the contested decision does not deprive them of all probative value.

1540 Fourth, in so far as the applicant contests that it concealed the anti-competitive nature of its practices, the Court observes that the Commission mentions in that regard, at recitals 1742 and 1743 of the contested decision, the following:

- an email of Mr I2, [confidential] of Intel, to [confidential] of Lenovo of 18 June 2006, in which he stated as follows: '[Mr L1] [confidential], [f] irst of all, the information in this note is incredibly sensitive and would be embarrassing to me and Intel if it was known. I am asking you as a matter of trust to read it and delete it with no sharing to your team. ... any meet-comp program that we may have had with Dell will get nullified as they introduce competition — this opens vistas of opportunity for Lenovo/Intel that I have only hinted at in the past ...';
- the secret nature of the exclusivity agreement between the applicant and MSH, and how the applicant insisted on this;
- the existence of rebate agreements that contained unwritten anti-competitive clauses as regards HP;
- the applicant's attempts to portray its conduct in a non-suspicious manner through the use of euphemisms.

1541 As regards, in the first place, the email of 18 June 2006, the applicant argues that this email merely reflects a negotiating effort by its [confidential] aimed at persuading Lenovo to give Intel more business. Obviously, it would have been embarrassing to Intel if it had become known to a third party, especially to Dell, that the applicant was using Dell's switch as a negotiating point with another OEM. The Court considers that that argument is not convincing. In the light of the statement that any meet-competition program would get nullified as Dell was introducing competition, the email provides evidence of the fact that the rebates granted by the applicant to Dell were conditioned on exclusivity (see paragraphs 460, 463, 1124 above). In addition, Mr I2's statement that the breach, by Dell, of that condition 'opens vistas of opportunities for Lenovo/Intel ... only hinted at in the past' meant that, following the reduction of the rebates granted to Dell, the applicant would offer Lenovo the preferential status Dell had had (see recital 526 of the contested decision). Consequently, Mr I2's request to [confidential] of Lenovo to delete the email is an indication that he sought to conceal the anti-competitive nature of the applicant's relationships with Dell and Lenovo.

1542 As regards, in the second place, the secret nature of the exclusivity agreement concluded with MSH, it has been demonstrated in more detail in paragraphs 1490 to 1492 above that a non-exclusivity clause was inserted in the exclusivity agreements, so that the contribution agreements stipulated the opposite of what was actually agreed.

1543 As regards, in the third place, the use of unwritten anti-competitive clauses vis-à-vis HP, the applicant merely claims that HP was not contractually bound by exclusivity obligations or other unwritten requirements. However, the unwritten conditions of the HPA agreements did not need to be legally binding to be capable of creating an incentive for HP to comply with them (see paragraph 106 above). Given that the contested decision correctly found that the rebates granted under the HPA agreements were subject to several unwritten anti-competitive conditions (see paragraphs 666 to 873 below), the unwritten nature of the clauses is also indicative of the manner in which the applicant attempted to conceal its anti-competitive practices.

1544 As regards, in the fourth place, the applicant's use of euphemisms, it should be noted, first of all, that the Commission concluded, at recital 661 of the contested decision, that the applicant used the acronym 'VOC', which stands for 'vendor of choice', in a series of documents as a euphemism to refer to MSH being bound to Intel by an exclusivity condition. The Commission specifies, at recital 662 of the contested decision, that there was also a 'Sales and Marketing Creation Reference Card', drawn up by Intel's Legal Department. In that document, under the heading 'Sensitive language', the term 'vendor of choice' was suggested to replace wording implying potentially inappropriate conduct as regards exclusivity:

'Avoid ALL militaristic, aggressive language ANYWHERE (including internal mail, memos…) e.g. erect barriers, …exclude from competition … War …Battle …Tie …Leverage …dominate …Top to Bottom …Squash … blow away the competition …be a killer …bundle …technology treadmill Use instead: lead the field …set the specifications …grow the market segment …be the vendor of choice …build upon …add value.'

1545 Second, recital 1743 of the contested decision mentions a series of emails of 30 April 2004. According to that decision, an Intel Germany executive referred to attempts that had been made by Intel to 'successfully inhibit further Opteron implementation in our key accounts'. An Intel France executive replied to that email as follows: '[P]lease be very careful using expressions like "inhibit further Opteron implementation" which could be misinterpreted as anti-competitive — I think you mean "win with IA vs Opteron" — If you see others use similar expressions please remind them of the current investigations by EU_FTC / dawn raids etc.' The contested decision specifies that that communication predates the inspections by the Commission.

1546 The applicant admits that it has never denied that 'vendor of choice' may mean that a customer is sole-sourcing or sourcing predominantly from Intel. However, in the applicant's submission, there is nothing in the 'Sales and Marketing Creation Reference Card' that supports the Commission's interpretation that it implies some form of binding commitment. This card is simply a document to educate its business people to avoid using language which may be misinterpreted by competition authorities. As regards the email of 30 April 2004, the applicant states that the email's purpose was also merely to warn against using language that 'could be misinterpreted as anti-competitive', which is a legitimate effort.

1547 However, a distinction must be drawn between a situation in which an undertaking is careful to ensure that its lawful conduct is not misinterpreted by a competition authority and a situation in which an undertaking seeks to ensure that its anti-competitive practices are not detected. It is true that, for an undertaking, it is in principle legitimate to warn its employees against using language that could be misinterpreted by a competition authority. However, such an approach is an indication that an undertaking concealed the anti-competitive nature of its practices where the existence of those practices has been established by means of other evidence.

1548 Lastly, the applicant submits that the Commission only set out specific allegations of concealment as regards MSH, HP, and Lenovo. In that regard, it should be borne in mind that recitals 1742 and 1743 of the contested decision concern the evidence of the overall strategy and that items of evidence set out in paragraph 1539 above are cited in that paragraph as indicia. The Court finds that that evidence demonstrates to the requisite legal standard that the applicant attempted to conceal the anti-competitive nature of its conduct, at least as regards its relationships with Dell, HP, Lenovo and MSH. In order to establish that the applicant implemented an overall strategy aimed at foreclosing AMD from the market, the Commission was not required to demonstrate, in the contested decision, an effort to conceal in relation to each practice implemented, but was entitled to confine itself to setting out the evidence in relation to those four undertakings.

1549 Moreover, the items of evidence set out in the contested decision as indicia at recitals 1742 and 1743 are confirmed by the general finding made at recital 167 of that decision, according to which all Intel's practices had a common strand in that numerous deals between Intel and its customers, sometimes worth hundreds of millions or even billions of USD, were made on the basis of handshake agreements or contained significant provisions which were unwritten. The complaint that the applicant used unwritten anti-competitive clauses is not only directed against the applicant's conduct vis-à-vis Dell, HP, Lenovo and MSH, but extends to the applicant's conduct vis-à-vis all the OEMs and MSH.

1550 It is true that the applicant submits that, in the CPU market, which is characterised by the rapid introduction of new products and significant price declines for existing products, informal agreements are a consequence of industry's pace and the demands of OEMs themselves. However, it must be stated that, although undertakings are free to conclude informally agreements which are consistent with the competition rules, recourse to informal anti-competitive conditions may constitute an indication of an effort to conceal such conditions. In the present case, such an indication stems not only from the informal nature of the agreements concluded between the applicant and the OEMs or MSH in itself, but, at least as regards HP and Lenovo, from the use of unwritten anti-competitive clauses which did not appear in the written contracts, or even, as regards MSH, from written terms which indicated the opposite of what was actually agreed.

1551 On the basis of the considerations set out in paragraphs 1540 to 1550 above, it is permissible to conclude that the Commission demonstrated to the requisite legal standard that the applicant attempted to conceal the anti -competitive nature of its practices. Consequently, it is not necessary to adjudicate also on the admissibility or the merits of the Commission's other arguments as regards whether other evidence exists which strengthens the abovementioned evidence or demonstrates more specifically that the applicant also disclosed its anti-competitive practices regarding Acer and NEC.

1552 On the basis of all the foregoing considerations, the Court therefore finds that the Commission proved to the requisite legal standard that the applicant implemented a long-term comprehensive strategy to foreclose AMD from the strategically most important sales channels.

III – The heads of claim for annulment or reduction of the fine

1553 According to Article 2 of the operative part of the contested decision, a fine of EUR 1.06 billion was imposed on the applicant.

1554 Pursuant to point 19 of the 2006 Guidelines, the Commission determined that the basic amount of the fine is related to a proportion of the value of sales, depending on the degree of gravity of the infringement, multiplied by the number of years of infringement (see recital 1778 of the contested decision).

1555 The Commission set at EUR 3 876 827 021 the value of sales to be considered, which represents the value of sales of x86 CPUs invoiced by Intel to undertakings established in the EEA market during the last year of the infringement (see recitals 1773 to 1777 of the contested decision).

1556 As regards the gravity of the infringement, the Commission took into account, in particular, the nature of the infringement, the market share of the parties concerned and the geographic scope of the infringement. The Commission also took into account the fact that Intel had committed a single infringement, that the intensity of that single infringement differed across the years and that most of the individual abuses concerned were concentrated in the period ranging from 2002 to 2005, that the abuses differed in their respective likely anti-competitive impact, and that Intel took measures to conceal the practices established in the contested decision. In consequence, the Commission fixed that proportion at 5% (see recitals 1779 to 1786 of that decision).

1557 Regarding the duration of the infringement, the Commission found that the abuse commenced in October 2002 and continued until at least December 2007. It therefore lasted 5 years and 3 months, which, in accordance with point 24 of the 2006 Guidelines, means the basic amount should be multiplied by 5.5 to take account of that duration (see recitals 1787 and 1788 of the contested decision).

1558 In view of the foregoing, the Commission found that the basic amount of the fine to impose on Intel was to be EUR 1 060 000 000 (see recital

1789 of the contested decision). It found no mitigating or aggravating circumstances (see recitals 1790 to 1801 of that decision).

1559 The applicant, supported by ACT, submits that, in light of the Court's unlimited jurisdiction pursuant to Article 261 TFEU and Article 31 of Regulation No 1/2003, the fine should be annulled or reduced substantially on the following grounds. First, the Commission misapplied the 2006 Guidelines and took irrelevant considerations into account. Second, Intel did not infringe Article 82 EC intentionally or through negligence. Third, the level of the fine is manifestly disproportionate.

A – The alleged incorrect application of the 2006 Guidelines and the alleged taking into account of irrelevant considerations

1560 The applicant claims that the calculation of the basic amount of the fine is vitiated by a number of flaws. First, the Commission failed properly to assess the goods or services to which the infringement relates between January and September 2006. The Commission moreover inflated the amount of the fine by using the value of Intel's sales in all EEA Member States in December 2007, whereas 12 Member States joined the EEA during the infringement period. Second, the Commission erroneously took into account concealment as a factor in assessing the gravity of the infringement. Third, the Commission erroneously used its finding of a single infringement as an aggravating factor across the whole time period. Fourth, the contested decision was incorrect in so far as the Commission applied a multiplier of 5.5 for duration to each infringement. Fifth, the Commission applied its guidelines retroactively.

1561 As a preliminary point, it should be noted that, at recitals 1747 and 1748 of the contested decision, the Commission was right to infer the existence of a single and continuous infringement of Article 82 EC, extending from October 2002 to December 2007 and aimed at foreclosing competitors from the market, from evidence of the existence of a comprehensive strategy to foreclose AMD from the strategically most important sales channels (see paragraphs 1523 to 1552 above).

1562 It is apparent from the case-law that the concept of a single and continuous infringement relates to a series of actions which form part of an overall plan because their identical object distorts competition within the common market. For the purposes of characterising various instances of conduct as a single and continuous infringement, it is necessary to establish whether they complement each other inasmuch as each of them is intended to deal with one or more consequences of the normal pattern of competition and, by interacting, contribute to the realisation of the objectives intended within the framework of that overall plan. In that regard, it will be necessary to take into account any circumstance capable of establishing or casting doubt on that complementary link, such as the period of application, the content (including the methods used) and, correlatively, the objective of the various actions in question (AstraZeneca, paragraph 64 above, paragraph 892).

1563 The Court observes that the findings of the contested decision relating to the existence of an overall strategy fulfil those requirements. Consequently, the Commission was entitled to infer from those findings that the applicant committed a single and continuous infringement. In that regard, the Court draws attention in particular to the consistency over time of the infringements at issue in the contested decision and their comparability and complementarity. The individual practices alleged against the applicant pursued an identical object since they were all aimed at foreclosing AMD from the worldwide market for x86 CPUs. In that regard, they were complementary in so far as those practices were applied to two levels of the distribution chain and in so far as the naked restrictions constituted tactical moves to foreclose AMD from well-identified specific products or sales channels, while exclusivity rebates and payments constituted more strategic devices to foreclose AMD from entire segments of OEMs' demand. Moreover, it should be recalled, in particular, that the coherence between the individual infringements is not interrupted by the fact that the infringements concerning Lenovo and MSH were less significant than the infringements concerning Dell and HP (see paragraphs 1525 to 1537 above).

1564 According to the case-law, the Commission was therefore entitled to impose a single fine. In that regard, the Commission was not required to state specifically in the grounds of the contested decision how it took into account each of the components of the abuse for the purposes of setting the fine (see, to that effect, Case T-83/91 Tetra Pak v Commission [1994] ECR II-755, paragraph 236, and Michelin II, paragraph 75 above, paragraph 265).

1565 It is in the light of the foregoing considerations that it is necessary to verify the applicant's arguments relating to the alleged incorrect application of the 2006 Guidelines.

1. The argument alleging erroneous assessment of the products to which the infringement relates between January and September 2006 and that the Commission ignored the fact that 12 Member States formed part of the EEA only during a part of the infringement period

1566 First, the applicant submits that the fine was unlawful because the 5% per annum figure was applied to too large a turnover figure between January and September 2006. The Commission failed to define a relevant product and geographic market in respect of the MSH allegations. Given that the alleged abuse in respect of MSH is the only infringement with a potential connection to the EEA from January 2006 until at least September 2006, the Commission erred in applying turnover in respect of the whole of the x86 CPU market in the EEA to an allegation which does not relate to that market. The Commission committed a manifest error of assessment in failing to take into account the limited geographic scope of the alleged infringement during this period in calculating the fine. MSH was not active in many Member States within the EEA and retail markets are likely to be no more than national in scope.

1567 Second, the applicant complains that the Commission inflated the fine by finding, at recital 1784 of the contested decision, that 'the whole EEA was covered by the unlawful conduct', and by using the value of Intel's sales in all EEA Member States in December 2007, that is to say, when the infringement period ended. However, 12 Member States joined the EEA during the infringement period and had not previously been subject to the Commission's jurisdiction. Had the Decision imposed a separate fine for each infringement, it would have had to exclude the value of Intel's sales in those states or apply a lower multiplier.

1568 Those arguments are not convincing.

1569 First, in accordance with point 13 of the 2006 Guidelines, in determining the basic amount of the fine to be imposed, the Commission will take the value of the undertaking's sales of goods or services to which the infringement directly or indirectly relates in the relevant geographic area within the EEA. That wording covers sales in the relevant market

(Case T-211/08 Putters International v Commission [2011] ECR II-3729, paragraph 59). Also according to point 13, the Commission will normally take the sales made by the undertaking during the last full business year of its participation in the infringement.

1570 Second, it follows from point 22 of the 2006 Guidelines that the geographic scope of the infringement is one of the factors that may be taken into consideration in order to determine the gravity of the infringement and therefore to decide whether the proportion of the value of sales to be considered should be at the lower end or at the higher end of the scale of 30% laid down in point 21 of the 2006 Guidelines.

1571 Although it is therefore true that both point 13 and point 21 of the 2006 Guidelines refer to the geographic scope of an infringement, the Court finds — as will be explained below — that, in the present case, the Commission did not infringe either point 13 of the 2006 Guidelines or point 21 thereof by failing to take into consideration both the geographic scope of the market on which MSH operated and the fact that 12 Member States formed part of the EEA only during part of the infringement period.

a) The existence of an infringement of point 13 of the 2006 Guidelines

1572 It is apparent from recitals 792 to 836 of the contested decision that the Commission concluded that the relevant market was the worldwide market for x86 CPUs. According to recital 1773 of that decision, the amount of EUR 3 876 827 021, on which the Commission relied as the value of sales to be taken into consideration, represents the value of sales of x86 CPUs invoiced by Intel to companies located in the EEA during the last year of the infringement. That value does not take account either of the alleged narrower geographic scope of the market on which MSH operated or of the fact that 12 Member States formed part of the EEA only during a part of the infringement period.

1573 However, the Court finds that, by failing to take into consideration both the geographic scope of the market on which MSH operated and the enlargement of the European Union during the infringement period, the Commission did not apply point 13 of the 2006 Guidelines incorrectly.

1574 In that regard, it should be recalled that, in the present case, the Commission was entitled to impose a single fine and that it was not required to state specifically how it took into account each of the components of the abuse for the purposes of setting the fine (see paragraph 1564 above).

1575 First, it should be noted that, in accordance with point 13 of the 2006 Guidelines, the year which is normally relevant for determining the value of sales is the last full business year of the participation in the infringement, namely, in the present case, 2007. The applicant does not claim that the Commission ought to have departed from that rule and chosen another year as reference year. However, for the whole of 2007, the Commission established the existence of an abuse not only in relation to MSH, but also in relation to Lenovo. As regards the applicant's conduct vis-à-vis Lenovo in 2007, the applicant does not contest that the relevant market was the worldwide market for x86 CPUs. Given that at least one of the abusive practices committed by the applicant in 2007 related therefore to the worldwide market for x86 CPUs, the Commission did not apply its guidelines incorrectly in so far as it set the value of sales by reference solely to the market for x86 CPUs, and not to the allegedly more limited consumer computer market on which MSH operated.

1576 In any event, it should be recalled that the Commission was not required to define a separate product market or a separate geographic market as regards MSH and that the applicant's practices vis-à-vis MSH were capable of restricting competition on the worldwide market for x86 CPUs (see paragraph 1533 above). Given that the Commission was not required to define a separate geographic market as regards MSH, nor was the Commission required to take account of the limited geographic scope of such a hypothetical market when setting the value of sales, in accordance with point 13 of the 2006 Guidelines.

1577 Second, the Court notes that the 12 Member States which joined the EEA during the infringement period formed part of the EEA during the entirety of 2007. Given that, in accordance with point 13 of the 2006 Guidelines, the relevant year for the calculation of the value of sales is, in the present case, 2007, the Commission was not required to take into consideration, when setting the amount of the value of sales, the fact that those Member States formed part of the EEA only during a part of the infringement period.

b) The existence of an infringement of point 21 of the 2006 Guidelines

1578 The Court notes that, as regards the gravity of the infringement, the Commission found, at recital 1784 of the contested decision, that the applicant's exclusionary strategy against AMD was worldwide in scope. For the purposes of assessing the gravity of the infringement, this means that the whole of the EEA was covered by the infringement.

1579 The Court finds that, by failing in this way to take into consideration the geographic scope of the market on which MSH operated, the Commission did not apply point 13 of the 2006 Guidelines incorrectly.

1580 The mere fact that, for a part of 2006, the contested decision finds only one illegal practice vis-à-vis MSH cannot call in question the conclusion that the applicant's exclusionary strategy against AMD was worldwide in scope. It should be recalled that the Commission was not required to define a separate product market or a separate geographic market as regards MSH and that the applicant's practices vis-à-vis MSH were capable of restricting competition on the worldwide market for x86 CPUs (see paragraph 1533 above). Moreover, since the applicant's practices vis-à-vis MSH were part of a coherent overall strategy, they cannot be considered in isolation. The geographic scope of that strategy was worldwide. Consequently, in the contested decision, the Commission correctly concluded that the whole of the EEA was covered by the infringement.

1581 Moreover, the Court finds that the Commission was also not required to take account of the fact that 12 Member States formed part of the EEA only during a part of the infringement period when, for the purposes of assessing the gravity of the infringement, it considered that the worldwide scope of the exclusionary strategy against AMD meant that the whole of the EEA had been covered by the infringement.

1582 It should be noted that the Commission found merely that the whole of the EEA had been covered by the infringement. Thus, it was referring in a dynamic manner to the States which formed part of the EEA at a given point during the infringement period. The Commission was not required to break down the geographic scope taken into consideration when assessing the gravity of a single infringement in step with the various States which joined the EEA at a given point during the infringement period. The Commission was not required to state specifically how it took into account each of the components of the abuse for the purposes of setting the fine (see paragraph 1564 above).

2. The taking into consideration of the concealment of the infringements

1583 It should be noted that, in order to assess the gravity of the infringement, the Commission, at recital 1785 of the contested decision, took account of the fact that the applicant took measures to conceal the practices at issue in that decision.

1584 The applicant claims that the Commission was wrong to take account of the alleged concealment of the infringement, given that it did not succeed in proving that concealment. In addition, the Commission's claims concerning that concealment relate only to MSH, HP and Lenovo and should not therefore be applied globally to all the infringements.

1585 Those arguments cannot succeed.

1586 As a preliminary point, it should be noted that the secret nature of an infringement of the competition rules of the European Union is a factor liable to exacerbate its gravity (see, to that effect, Joined Cases T-259/02 to T-264/02 and T-271/02 Raiffeisen Zentralbank Österreich and Others v Commission [2006] ECR II-5169, paragraph 252, and Imperial Chemical Industries v Commission, paragraph 139 above, paragraph 446). In the present case, the Commission took into account Intel's attempts to conceal its conduct, among many other factors, when assessing the gravity of the infringement.

1587 It should be recalled that the evidence relied on in the contested decision demonstrates to the requisite legal standard that the applicant attempted to conceal the anti-competitive nature of its conduct, at least as regards its relationships with Dell, HP, Lenovo and MSH (see paragraphs 1540 to 1551 above). Contrary to the applicant's claim, it was sufficient that the Commission set out specific allegations of concealment only as regards those four undertakings in order to take into consideration concealment as one of the factors determining the gravity of the single infringement. The Commission was not required to state specifically how it took into account each of the components of the abuse for the purposes of setting the fine (see paragraph 1564 above).

3. The aggravating nature of the finding of a single infringement

1588 It should be noted that, at recital 1747 of the contested decision, in the context of the findings concerning the existence of an overall strategy, the Commission concluded that, taken together, the applicant's individual practices were capable of having or likely to have had an even greater impact on the market. At recital 1785 of that decision, in the context of the findings relating to the gravity of the infringement, the Commission stated that it had taken into account the fact that Intel had committed a single infringement, that the intensity of that single infringement had differed across the years, that most of the individual abuses concerned were concentrated in the period ranging from 2002 to 2005 and that the abuses differed in their respective likely anti-competitive impact.

1589 The applicant claims that the Commission 'presumably' used the finding of a single infringement as an aggravating factor in determining the gravity. The application of a single infringement as a factor increasing the gravity of the infringement is incorrect, because, for certain periods, it cannot be shown that 'such' a 'factor' could increase the gravity of the alleged conduct. For part of 2006, when the only conduct relating to the EEA involved MSH, there can be no basis for attributing greater gravity to Intel's conduct resulting from a single infringement.

1590 Those arguments must be rejected.

1591 It should be recalled that, in the present case, the Commission was entitled to impose a single fine and that it was not required to state specifically how it took into account each of the components of the abuse for the purposes of setting the fine (see paragraph 1564 above). Moreover, the applicant's argument is based on the incorrect premiss that the Commission increased the gravity of the unlawful conduct to be taken into account on account of the existence of a single infringement. That, however, is not the case. The Commission considered that the intensity of the single infringement differed across the years, that most of the individual abuses concerned were concentrated in the period ranging from 2002 to 2005 and that the abuses differed in their respective likely anti-competitive impact. Those findings take account, to the requisite legal standard, of the fact that, for part of 2006, the infringement involving MSH was the only infringement in relation to the EEA which was established in the contested decision.

4. The application of a multiplier of 5.5 for the duration of the infringement

1592 It should be observed that, regarding the duration of the infringement, the Commission found, at recitals 1787 and 1788 of the contested decision, that the abuse commenced in October 2002 and continued until at least December 2007. It therefore lasted 5 years and 3 months, which, in accordance with point 24 of the 2006 Guidelines, means the basic amount should be multiplied by 5.5 to take account of that duration.

1593 In the applicant's submission, the contested decision is incorrect in so far as the Commission applied a multiplier of 5.5 for duration to each infringement. This approach operated to its detriment, as each of the infringements in relation to the OEMs was of significantly shorter duration than the overall infringement period.

1594 That argument is not convincing.

1595 Contrary to the applicant's claim, the Commission did not apply a multiplier of 5.5 to each of the individual infringements, but to the single infringement. Since the Commission correctly found the existence of a single infringement from October 2002 to December 2007 (see paragraphs 1561 to 1563 above), that approach cannot be criticised.

5. The retroactive application of the 2006 Guidelines

1596 The applicant claims that the Commission infringed the principles of non-retroactivity and the protection of legitimate expectations by applying the 2006 Guidelines retroactively. The replacement of certain guidelines by other guidelines must be distinguished from the first introduction of the guidelines. The first introduction of the guidelines created for the first time a legitimate expectation which until then had not existed, which prevents the application of new guidelines retroactively.

1597 That argument cannot be accepted.

1598 It is apparent from the case-law that neither the principle of legal certainty nor the principle that offences and punishments are to be strictly defined by law, which is enshrined in Article 7(1) of the ECHR, precludes the Commission from deciding to adopt and apply new guidelines on the method of setting fines, even after the infringement has been committed. The interest in effective enforcement of the competition rules justifies that, within the limits laid down in Article 23 of Regulation No 1/2003, an undertaking must take account of the possibility of a modification to the general competition policy of the Commission as regards fines with respect both to the method of calculation and the level of fines (judgment of 2 February 2012 in Case T-83/08 Denki Kagaku Kogyo and Denka Chemicals v Commission, not published in the ECR, paragraphs 98 to 127). That finding also holds true with respect to Article 49(1) of the Charter of Fundamental Rights. The Commission was therefore, a fortiori, entitled to apply its 2006 Guidelines to a single infringement which ended only after those guidelines were adopted.

B – The alleged absence of an intentional or negligent infringement of Article 82 EC

1599 The applicant claims that it did not act negligently. In order to substantiate that assertion, it submits, in essence, that conditional rebates are not always unlawful and that naked restrictions constitute a new category of abuse. It showed that the Commission failed to establish the existence of a strategy to foreclose AMD. The Commission erred in taking the view that Intel took steps to conceal its conduct. The applicant could not have foreseen the results that were reached by the Commission in the application of the AEC test. Those results are based upon internal data from the various OEMs which was neither known nor accessible to Intel.

1600 Those arguments cannot succeed.

1601 It is settled case-law that the condition that the infringement was committed intentionally or negligently is satisfied where the undertaking concerned cannot be unaware of the anti-competitive nature of its conduct, whether or not it was aware that it was infringing the competition rules of the Treaty (Tetra Pak v Commission, paragraph 1564 above, paragraph 238, and Case T-271/03 Deutsche Telekom v Commission [2008] ECR II-477, paragraph 295). An undertaking is aware of the anti-competitive nature of its conduct where it is aware of the essential facts justifying both the finding of a dominant position on the relevant market and the finding by the Commission of an abuse of that position (see, to that effect, Michelin I, paragraph 74 above, paragraph 107, and Raiffeisen Zentralbank Österreich and Others v Commission, paragraph 1586 above, paragraphs 207 and 210; see, also Opinion of Advocate General Mazák in Case C-280/08 P Deutsche Telekom, paragraph 98 above, point 39).

1602 As regards, first, the argument that conditional rebates are not always unlawful and that naked restrictions constitute a new category of abuse, it is sufficient to note that such a line of argument is merely intended to show that the applicant was unaware that the conduct complained of in the decision at issue was unlawful in the light of Article 82 EC. That line of argument must therefore be rejected in accordance with the case-law cited in the previous paragraph (see, by analogy, Case C-280/08 P Deutsche Telekom, paragraph 98 above, paragraph 127). In any event, the applicant could not have been unaware of the anti-competitive nature of its conduct. The European Union Courts have censured on several occasions the implementation, by an undertaking in a dominant position, of practices consisting in the grant of financial incentives conditional upon exclusivity. In that regard, it is sufficient to refer to Hoffmann-La Roche, paragraph 71 above, and to Case C-310/93 P BPB Industries and British Gypsum, paragraph 89 above. As regards naked restrictions, it was held in paragraphs 219 and 220 above that the characterisation of such practices as abusive cannot be regarded as novel and that, in any event, the fact that conduct with the same features has not been examined in past decisions does not exonerate an undertaking.

1603 Second, it should be recalled that the evidence relied on in the contested decision demonstrates to the requisite legal standard that the applicant implemented a long-term comprehensive strategy to foreclose AMD from the strategically most important sales channels and that the applicant attempted to conceal the anti-competitive nature of its conduct, at least as regards its relationships with Dell, HP, Lenovo and MSH (see paragraphs 1523 to 1552 above). Consequently, it is permissible to conclude that the applicant committed the infringement established at least negligently.

1604 Third, it is necessary to reject the applicant's argument that it could not have foreseen the results that were reached by the Commission in the application of the AEC test. The Court notes that, in the contested decision, the Commission relied, primarily, on the criteria stemming from the Court's case-law in Hoffmann-La Roche, paragraph 71 above, in finding the exclusivity rebates to be unlawful (see paragraphs 69, 72 and 73 above). However, it based its contested decision only for the sake of completeness on the AEC test (see paragraphs 173 and 175 above). The Court recalls that the application of an AEC test is not necessary to establish the illegality of the applicant's practices and that such a test can also not provide a reliable means by which the dominant undertaking may rule out any infringement (see paragraphs 140 to 166 above). Even on the assumption that the applicant could not have foreseen the results that were reached by the Commission in applying that test, that would not call in question the fact that the applicant could not have been unaware of the essential facts justifying the finding by the Commission of an abuse of its dominant position according to the criteria stemming from the case-law in Hoffmann-La Roche, paragraph 71 above.

C – The allegedly disproportionate nature of the fine

1605 The applicant relies, in essence, on three arguments to support its assertion that the level of the fine was disproportionate. The fine was not imposed by an independent authority. The fine is disproportionate in relation to fines imposed in other decisions. The imposition of the highest fine ever imposed is disproportionate in the light of the absence of actual effects of the infringement on the market.

1606 All those arguments must be rejected.

1. The argument alleging the Commission's lack of independence

1607 In the applicant's submission, the Commission is not an independent and impartial tribunal within the meaning of the ECHR. The applicant claims that, since the fine is criminal in nature, in the sense of Article 6 of the ECHR, it was imposed unlawfully and in violation of Intel's right to have the charge against it decided by an independent tribunal.

1608 That argument cannot be accepted.

1609 The right of access to an independent and impartial tribunal, on which the applicant relies, is one of the guarantees enshrined in Article 6(1) of the ECHR. In EU law, the protection afforded by that article is guaranteed by Article 47 of the Charter of Fundamental Rights. It is therefore appropriate to refer only to Article 47 (see, to that effect Case C-386/10 P Chalkor v Commission [2011] ECR I-13085. paragraph 51). Article 52(3) of the Charter of Fundamental Rights states that, in so far as the Charter contains rights which correspond to those guaranteed by the ECHR, their meaning and scope are to be the same as those laid down by the ECHR. According to the explanation of that provision, which must be taken into account by the Courts of the European Union in accordance with Article 52(7) of the Charter of Fundamental Rights, the meaning and the scope of the guaranteed rights are to be determined not only by reference to the text of the ECHR, but also, inter alia, by reference to the case-law of the European Court of Human Rights (see, to that effect, Case C-279/09 DEB [2010] ECR I-13849, paragraph 35).

1610 It follows from the case-law of the European Court of Human Rights that Article 6(1) of the ECHR does not preclude a 'penalty' from being imposed by an administrative authority in the first instance. For this to be possible, however, decisions taken by administrative authorities which do not themselves satisfy the requirements laid down in Article 6(1) of the ECHR must be subject to subsequent review by a judicial body that has full jurisdiction. The characteristics of a judicial body that has full jurisdiction include the power to quash in all respects, on questions of fact and law, the decision of the body below. The judicial body must in particular have jurisdiction to examine all questions of fact and law relevant to the dispute before it (see judgment of the European Court of Human Rights in A. Menarini Diagnostics S.R.L. v. Italy, no. 43509/08, 27 September 2011, § 59).

1611 It may be inferred from that case-law that the fact that the Commission acts as investigator, prosecutor and adjudicator in procedures relating to infringements of the competition rules laid down in Regulation No 1/2003 is not of itself incompatible with Article 47 of the Charter of Fundamental Rights, provided, however, that the undertakings subject to such procedures have a right to appeal the Commission's decision before a body which satisfies the requirements under Article 47 (Opinion of Advocate General Mengozzi in Case C-521/09 P Elf Aquitaine v Commission [2011] ECR I-8947, point 31).

1612 In that regard, it is clear from the case-law that the review of legality provided for under Article 263 TFEU, supplemented by the unlimited jurisdiction in respect of the amount of the fine, provided for under Article 31 of Regulation No 1/2003, in accordance with Article 261 TFEU, meets the requirements of the principle of effective judicial protection in Article 47 of the Charter of Fundamental Rights. The review provided for by the Treaties involves review by the Courts of the European Union of both the law and the facts, and means that they have the power to assess the evidence, to annul the contested decision and to alter the amount of a fine (see, to that effect, Chalkor v Commission, paragraph 1609 above, paragraph 67).

2. The disproportionate nature of the fine in relation to other fines

1613 The applicant claims that the fine imposed upon Intel is also disproportionate compared to other recent cases including the case giving rise to the judgment in Case T-201/04 Microsoft v Commission [2007] ECR II-3601.

1614 It is clear from settled case-law that the Commission's practice in previous decisions does not itself serve as a legal framework for the fines imposed in competition matters and that decisions in other cases can give only an indication for the purpose of determining whether there might be discrimination since the facts of those cases, such as markets, products, the undertakings and periods concerned, are not likely to be the same (Case C-167/04 P JCB Service v Commission [2006] ECR I-8935, paragraphs 201 and 205, and Case C-76/06 P Britannia Alloys & Chemicals v Commission [2007] ECR I-4405, paragraph 60; Case T-192/06 Caffaro v Commission [2011] ECR II-3063, paragraph 46).

1615 Nevertheless, observance of the principle of equal treatment, which prevents comparable situations from being treated differently and different situations from being treated in the same way, unless such difference in treatment is objectively justified, is incumbent on the Commission when it imposes a fine on an undertaking for infringement of the competition rules, as it is on any institution in carrying out all its activities. However, previous decisions by the Commission imposing fines can be relevant from the point of view of observance of the principle of equal treatment only where it is demonstrated that the facts of the cases in those other decisions, such as markets, products, the countries, the undertakings and periods concerned, are comparable to those of the present case (Case T-360/09 E.ON Ruhrgas and E.ON v Commission [2012] ECR, paragraphs 261 and 262 and the case-law cited).

1616 In the present case, the applicant has failed to demonstrate that the facts of the case in the previous decisions on which it relies are comparable to those of the present case. Consequently, in the light of the case-law cited in paragraph 1615 above, those decisions are not relevant from the point of view of observance of the principle of equal treatment.

1617 With respect, first, to the case giving rise to Microsoft v Commission, paragraph 1613 above, the applicant merely notes the difference between that case and the present case, claiming that, in that case, the conduct at issue resulted in multiple and measurable negative effects on competitors, which is not the situation in the present case. However, the applicant does not put forward any argument to demonstrate that the facts of the case which gave rise to Microsoft v Commission are comparable to those of the present case. The Court observes that that case concerned inter alia markets and abusive practices different from those at issue in the present case.

1618 Second, the applicant relies on the Commission Decision of 12 November 2008 relating to a proceeding under Article 81 [EC] and Article 53 of the EEA Agreement (Case COMP/39.125 — Car glass), a summary of which was published in the Official Journal of 25 July 2009 (OJ 2009 C 173, p. 13), in support of its argument that the fine imposed on it is considerably larger than the highest ever cartel fine imposed on a recidivist. However, the applicant fails to demonstrate that the facts of the case which gave rise to that decision, which related to a cartel and not to an abuse of a dominant position, are comparable to those of the present case.

1619 Third, as regards the comparison of the fine imposed in the present case with those imposed in the cases which gave rise to Hoffmann-La Roche, paragraph 71 above, Michelin I, paragraph 74 above, Michelin II, paragraph 75 above, and Case T-219/99 British Airways, paragraph 186 above, the Court finds that the applicant has also failed to demonstrate that the facts of those cases are comparable to those of the present case. In that regard, first, the Court would point out that Michelin I, paragraph 74 above, Michelin II, paragraph 75 above, and Case T-219/99 British Airways, paragraph 186 above, did not relate to exclusivity rebates, but to rebates falling within the third category (see paragraph 78 above) and that the present case also relates to naked restrictions. Second, it should be stressed that, on the assumption that the types of abuse at issue in the present case are similar, or even identical, to those at issue in the cases which gave rise to Hoffmann-La Roche, paragraph 71 above, Michelin I, paragraph 74 above, Michelin II, paragraph 75 above, and Case T-219/99 British Airways, paragraph 186 above, that cannot however suffice to make the present case and those relied on by the applicant comparable for the purposes of the case-law cited in paragraph 1615 above, in the light of the differences between those cases as regards in particular the undertakings, the relevant markets and goods and of the time lapse between those cases and the evolution of the Commission's fining policy.

3. The need to demonstrate that the infringement had actual effects

1620 It should be recalled that, in order to determine the gravity of the infringement, the Commission took into account inter alia the nature of the infringement, the market share of the undertakings concerned and the geographic scope of the infringement. As regards in particular the nature of the infringement, the Commission found, at recital 1780 of the contested decision, that the x86 CPU market is of great economic importance. According to that decision, that market generated revenues above USD 30 billion in 2007. This means that any anti-competitive conduct on that market had a considerable impact.

1621 The applicant submits that the level of the fine is based upon the alleged 'considerable impact' on the market, but that no analysis of the actual effects of the alleged abusive conduct on AMD, or the market, has been carried out. The applicant points out that its fine of EUR 1.06 billion is the highest fine ever imposed on a single company for an infringement of the competition rules. It was therefore necessary, in assessing that fine, to consider the actual effects of the infringement and the causal link between those effects and the injury to consumers or competitors, regardless of whether actual effects are relevant to the finding of an abuse. The applicant claims that the evidence demonstrates that, during the relevant period, the market for CPUs was characterised by intense competition between AMD and Intel, which resulted in constantly falling prices and improving product quality, to the benefit of consumers. Moreover, AMD multiplied its market share. Lastly, an OEM's decision to buy the applicant's products was based if not entirely, then at least in part, on business reasons other than the loyalty-inducing effects of the conditional rebates.

1622 Pursuant to Article 23(3) of Regulation No 1/2003, in fixing the amount of the fine, regard is to be had both to the gravity and to the duration of the infringement. It is clear from the case-law that the gravity of infringements of competition law must be assessed in the light of numerous factors, such as, inter alia, the particular circumstances of the case, its context and the dissuasive effect of fines, although no binding or exhaustive list of the criteria to be applied has been drawn up. In consequence, contrary to the applicant's assertion, the actual impact of the infringement on the market is not as a rule, according to the criteria established by the case-law, a factor which must be taken into account, but just one among a number of other factors to be taken into account in evaluating the gravity of the infringement and setting the amount of the fine (see, to that effect and by analogy, Case C-534/07 P Prym and Prym Consumer v Commission [2009] ECR I-7415, 'Prym', paragraphs 54 and 55). In addition, it is clear from the case-law that factors relating to the object of a course of conduct may be more significant for the purposes of setting the amount of the fine than those relating to its effects (AstraZeneca, paragraph 64 above, paragraph 902).

1623 Under the Guidelines on the method of setting fines imposed pursuant to Article 15(2) of Regulation No 17 and Article 65(5) of the [CS] Treaty (OJ 1998 C 9, p. 3) ('the 1998 Guidelines'), in assessing the gravity of the infringement, account had to be taken inter alia of 'its actual impact on the market, where this can be measured' (under Section 1.A.). In that regard, it was apparent from the case-law that, at least so far as concerned infringements which could be classified as very serious infringements solely on account of their nature, the actual impact of the infringement on the market was only an optional factor such as to allow the Commission to increase the starting amount of the fine beyond the minimum likely amount of EUR 20 million (see, to that effect, Prym, paragraph 1622 above, paragraph 75). It is true that it was also apparent from the case-law that, where the Commission considered it appropriate for the purposes of calculating the fine to take that optional element — the actual impact of the infringement on the market — into account, it could not just put forward a mere presumption but was required to provide specific, credible and adequate evidence with which to assess what actual influence the infringement may have had on competition in that market (Prym, paragraph 1622 above, paragraph 82).

1624 However, in the present case, the determination of the amount of the fine is not based on the 1998 Guidelines, but on the 2006 Guidelines. The Court would point out that, unlike the 1998 Guidelines, the 2006 Guidelines no longer provide for the 'actual impact on the market, where this can be measured' to be taken into account when the gravity of a given infringement is assessed. According to point 22 of the 2006 Guidelines, in order to decide whether the proportion of the value of sales determined by reference to the gravity should be at the lower end or at the higher end of the scale of up to 30%, the Commission will have regard to a number of factors, such as the nature of the infringement, the combined market share of all the undertakings concerned, the geographic scope of the infringement and whether or not the infringement has been implemented.

1625 It is therefore true that, according to the 2006 Guidelines, the Commission is not, as a general rule, obliged to take into consideration the actual impact of the infringement on the market when setting the proportion of the value of sales determined by reference to the gravity. However, the Court would point out that nor do the Guidelines preclude consideration of the actual impact of the infringement on the market in order to increase that proportion. In that regard, if the Commission considers it appropriate to take into account the actual impact of the infringement on the market in order to increase that proportion, the case-law cited in paragraph 1623 above also applies with respect to the 2006 Guidelines, so that the Commission must provide specific, credible and adequate evidence with which to assess what actual influence the infringement may have had on competition in that market. However, the Commission does not necessarily have to take account of the absence of any actual impact as an attenuating factor for the assessment of the gravity pursuant to point 22 of the 2006 Guidelines. It is sufficient that the level set by the Commission of the proportion of the value of sales to be taken into consideration is justified by other factors capable of influencing the determination of gravity.

1626 It is in the light of the foregoing considerations that the applicant's arguments must be assessed.

1627 First, it is necessary to reject the argument that the level of the fine is, in the present case, based upon the alleged 'considerable impact' on the market, but that no analysis of the actual effects of the alleged abusive conduct on AMD, or the market, has been carried out. It must be stated that, in the present case, the Commission did not take into consideration the actual impact of the infringement on the market in order to determine its gravity. Contrary to the applicant's claim, it may not be inferred from the fact that, in the contested decision, the Commission found that 'any anti-competitive behaviour on [the x86 CPU market] has a considerable impact', that the Commission took such an impact into consideration. The Court would point out in that regard that the finding criticised by the applicant was made by the Commission in order to describe the nature of the infringement. Since the 'nature' of an infringement refers to its abstract and general features, the Commission was entitled, in that context, to find that, in the light of the size of the revenues generated on the x86 CPU market, any anti-competitive conduct on that market has a considerable impact. In so doing, the Commission did not take into consideration the actual effects on the market of the practices at issue in the contested decision, but the 'nature' and therefore the capability of those practices to have such effects.

1628 The fact that the Commission did not take into consideration the actual impact of the infringement on the market in order to determine the amount of the fine is also confirmed by the following matters. On the one hand, whilst certain passages of the contested decision which do not refer to the determination of the amount of the fine contain conclusions relating to the actual impact of the applicant's conduct on the OEMs' and MSH's freedom of choice (see recitals 1001 and 1678 of that decision) and on the harm suffered by consumers (see recitals 1597 to 1616 of that decision), the Commission refrained from referring to those conclusions when determining the gravity of the infringement. On the other hand, in the conclusion on gravity, set out at recital 1785 of that decision, the Commission found that the abuses differed in their respective 'likely anti-competitive impact'. The fact that, in the conclusion on gravity, the Commission referred to the 'likely anti-competitive impact' of the individual abuses demonstrates unequivocally that it did not take into consideration the actual impact of the infringement on the market, but only its likely impact.

1629 The Court therefore holds that the Commission did not rely on the actual impact of the infringement in order to increase its gravity.

1630 Second, in so far as the applicant submits that the Commission was wrong not to take into account the absence of actual anti-competitive effects of the infringement and of a causal link between those effects and harm to consumers or competitors as an attenuating factor for the assessment of the gravity, its arguments must also be rejected. The Court finds that, in order to set the proportion of the value of sales determined by reference to the gravity of the infringement at 5%, the Commission was not required to take into consideration the alleged absence of any actual impact of the infringement on the market. In the present case, the other matters on which the Commission relied in the contested decision for the purposes of determining the gravity of the infringement justify the setting of the proportion of the value of sales to be taken into consideration at 5%.

1631 In that regard, it should be noted, as a preliminary point, that the level of 5% set in the contested decision is at the lower end of the scale, which, according to point 21 of the 2006 Guidelines, can go up to 30%.

1632 As regards, next, in the first place, the nature of the infringement, it should be noted that, at recitals 1780 and 1781 of the contested decision, the Commission considered that, besides the applicant, which had 80% market share, the only meaningful competitor on the market was AMD. The Commission also stated that the applicant implemented an overall strategy aimed at anti-competitively foreclosing AMD from the market. Thus, the applicant's abusive practices were aimed at foreclosing the only meaningful competitor or, at least, restricting its access to the market. In the light of the barriers to access to the production of x86 CPUs, it is likely that if AMD had been eliminated or marginalised, there would have been no credible entrant in the market.

1633 As regards, in the second place, the market share of the undertakings concerned, the Commission found, at recital 1783 of the contested decision, that during the entire infringement period the applicant not only held a dominant position in the x86 CPU market in all segments, but that its market share was also much higher than that of its competitors.

1634 As regards, in the third place, the geographic scope of the infringement, the Commission found, at recital 1784 of the contested decision, that the applicant's exclusionary strategy against AMD was worldwide in scope. For the purposes of assessing the gravity of the infringement, this means that the whole of the EEA was covered by the infringement (see paragraphs 1578 to 1582 above).

1635 In the fourth place, it should be recalled that, in the conclusion on the gravity of the infringement, the Commission, at recital 1785 of the contested decision, found inter alia that the applicant engaged in a single infringement the intensity of which differed across the years, that the individual abuses differed in their respective likely anti-competitive impact and that the applicant attempted to conceal the anti-competitive nature of its conduct (see paragraphs 1583 to 1591 above).

1636 Those findings, which are either not contested by the applicant or were established by the Commission to the requisite legal standard, are sufficient to justify setting the proportion of the value of sales at 5%.

1637 Third, as regards the applicant's arguments aimed at substantiating the absence of any actual effects on the market and of a causal link, it should be recalled, for the sake of completeness, that neither the growth in the market shares of AMD nor the decrease in the price of x86 CPUs over the period covered by the contested decision means that the applicant's practices had no effect. In the absence of those practices, it may legitimately be considered that the increase in the competitor's market share and the decrease in the price of x86 CPUs might have been greater (see paragraph 186 above). Similarly, in so far as the applicant relies on business reasons other than the loyalty-inducing effects of the conditional rebates for OEMs' decisions to buy its products, the Court finds that that line of argument is not such as to rule out any influence of the conditional rebates and payments at issue on the OEMs' commercial decisions (see paragraph 597 above).

4. Conclusion

1638 Accordingly, all the arguments by which the applicant seeks to establish that the level of the fine is disproportionate must be rejected.

D – The exercise of unlimited jurisdiction

1639 At the hearing, the applicant drew attention to four points justifying, in its submission, a reduction of the fine by the Court in the exercise of its unlimited jurisdiction. First, it draws attention to the complexity of the present case and submits that it was very difficult for it to comply with the law. In the present case, the Commission followed the approach of the Article 82 Guidance. That guidance does not prohibit conditional rebates per se, but requires the application of an AEC test. The lack of legal certainty thus generated should be taken into consideration by the Court. Second, the applicant pleads that the administrative procedure lasted nine years, whereas Article 6 of the ECHR and Article 41 of the Charter of Fundamental Rights require criminal cases to be dealt with expeditiously. A substantial part of the delay was caused by the work necessary for the application of the AEC test. Delay is a factor which the Court can always take into consideration. Third, the Court should take account of the Ombudsman's decision of 14 July 2009 finding that the failure to record the meeting between the Commission and Mr D1 constituted a case of maladministration. Fourth, with respect to the abuse concerning Acer, the Court should take account of the fact that there may have been a delay of only two to four weeks in launching the notebook.

1640 However, none of those arguments is capable of leading to an alteration of the amount of the fine set by the Commission.

1641 First, the applicant may not derive any benefit from the alleged legal uncertainty as regards the illegality of the exclusivity rebates. The Commission and the Court of Justice have censured on several occasions the implementation, by an undertaking in a dominant position, of practices consisting in the grant of financial incentives conditional upon exclusivity (see paragraph 1602 above). Regarding the Article 82 Guidance, it is apparent from recital 916 of the contested decision that the Commission did not apply that guidance in the present case. As was explained above, nor was the Commission required to do so. In addition, the applicant has failed to demonstrate that the Commission caused it to entertain a legitimate expectation as regards the application of the AEC test (see paragraphs 160 to 165 above).

1642 With respect, second, to the duration of the administrative procedure, the applicant's line of argument cannot succeed either.

1643 In that regard, it must be pointed out that the exercise of unlimited jurisdiction does not amount to a review of the Court's own motion, and that proceedings before the Courts of the European Union are inter partes. With the exception of pleas involving matters of public policy which the Courts are required to raise of their own motion, such as the failure to state reasons for a contested decision, it is for the applicant to raise pleas in law against that decision and to adduce evidence in support of those pleas (Chalkor v Commission, paragraph 1609 above, paragraph 64).

1644 The plea put forward by the applicant, which relates solely to the length of the administrative procedure and not to the length of the procedure before the Court, must be declared inadmissible under Article 48(2) of the Rules of Procedure. That plea, which was not put forward in the application, cannot be regarded as elaborating directly or by implication on a plea already put forward in the application and is not based on matters of law or of fact which came to light in the course of the procedure. Nor is there any need in the circumstances of this case for the Court to examine of its own motion the plea alleging that the procedure before the Commission was unreasonably long (see, by analogy, Case T-18/03 CD-Contact Data v Commission [2009] ECR II-1021, paragraph 130).

1645 As regards, third, the failure to record the meeting between the Commission and Mr D1, it was specified above that the Commission remedied the initial omission in the administrative procedure, stemming from the failure to draw up a succinct note and make it available to the applicant, by providing the applicant with the non-confidential version of the note to the file (see paragraph 622 above). Accordingly, it is not necessary to alter the amount of the fine. For the sake of completeness, it should be pointed out that, even if the procedural error had not been regularised, that irregularity would not be such as to result in the Court's altering the amount of the fine.

1646 Fourth, as regards the abuse concerning Acer, the applicant's argument, according to which the delay in launching the notebook concerned was, in fact, less than four months, was rejected in paragraphs 1345 to 1357 above.

1647 Moreover, it must be noted that having regard to the unlimited jurisdiction of the Court in relation to fines for infringement of the competition rules, there is nothing in the complaints, arguments or matters of law and of fact put forward by the applicant in connection with all the pleas examined above from which it might be concluded that the fine that was imposed on it by the contested decision is disproportionate. On the contrary, it must be held that the fine is appropriate to the circumstances of the case. In the context of that assessment, it is necessary inter alia to take into account the matters set out in paragraphs 1631 to 1636 above and the fact that the fine is equivalent to 4.15% of Intel's annual turnover, which is well below the 10% ceiling set in Article 23(2) of Regulation No 1/2003.

Costs

1648 Under the first subparagraph of Article 87(2) of the Rules of Procedure, the unsuccessful party is to be ordered to pay the costs if they have been applied for in the successful party's pleadings.

1649 Since the Commission has applied for costs and the applicant has been unsuccessful, the latter must be ordered to bear its own costs and to pay those incurred by the Commission, with the exception of the Commission's costs incurred in connection with the intervention of ACT. Moreover, the applicant must be ordered to pay UFC's costs, in accordance with the form of order sought by UFC.

1650 Since ACT has been unsuccessful, it must be ordered to bear its own costs and pay those incurred by the Commission in connection with its intervention, in accordance with the form of order sought by the Commission.

On those grounds,

THE GENERAL COURT (Seventh Chamber, Extended Composition)

hereby:

1. Dismisses the action;

2. Orders Intel Corp. to bear its own costs and to pay those incurred by the European Commission, with the exception of the Commission's costs incurred in connection with the intervention of the Association for Competitive Technology, Inc., and the costs incurred by Union fédérale des consommateurs — Que choisir (UFC — Que choisir);

3. Orders the Association for Competitive Technology to bear its own costs and to pay the Commission's costs incurred in connection with its intervention.

[Alfred] Dittrich

[Irena] Wiszniewska-Białecka

[Miro] Prek

[Juraj] Schwarcz

[Mariyana] Kancheva

Delivered in open court in Luxembourg on 12 June 2014.

[Signatures]

Table of contents

2.4) The argument alleging the relevance of the amount of the rebate

2.5) The argument based on the relevance of the duration

2.6) The argument based on the small part of the market concerned by the conduct complained of

2.7) The argument that the alleged exclusivity conditions did not cover a significant portion of certain OEMs' requirements

2.8) The argument based on customers' buying power

2.9) The line of argument concerning the relevance of the AEC test

b) The payments granted to MSH

c) Analysis of the capability of the rebates to restrict competition according to the circumstances of the case

3. The legal characterisation of the so-called 'naked restrictions'

B – The Commission's jurisdiction

1. Arguments of the parties

2. Findings of the Court

a) Preliminary observations

b) Qualified effects

1) Preliminary observations

2) Acer

2.1) Substantial effect

2.2) Immediate effect

2.3) Foreseeable effect

3) Lenovo

3.1) The naked restrictions

i) The postponement of the launch concerning the Chinese market

ii) The postponement of the launch concerning the worldwide market

3.2) The exclusivity rebates

c) Implementation

1) Acer

2) Lenovo

d) The effect on trade between Member States

C – Procedural irregularities

[omitted]

D – Errors of assessment concerning the practices relating to the various OEMs and MSH

[omitted]

E – The evidence of an overall strategy aimed at foreclosing AMD's access to the most important sales channels

III – The heads of claim for annulment or reduction of the fine

A – The alleged incorrect application of the 2006 Guidelines and the alleged taking into account of irrelevant considerations

1. The argument alleging erroneous assessment of the products to which the infringement relates between January and September 2006 and that the Commission ignored the fact that 12 Member States formed part of the EEA only during a part of the infringement period

a) The existence of an infringement of point 13 of the 2006 Guidelines

b) The existence of an infringement of point 21 of the 2006 Guidelines

2. The taking into consideration of the concealment of the infringements

3. The aggravating nature of the finding of a single infringement

4. The application of a multiplier of 5.5 for the duration of the infringement

5. The retroactive application of the 2006 Guidelines

B – The alleged absence of an intentional or negligent infringement of Article 82 EC

C – The allegedly disproportionate nature of the fine

1. The argument alleging the Commission's lack of independence

2. The disproportionate nature of the fine in relation to other fines

3. The need to demonstrate that the infringement had actual effects

4. Conclusion

D – The exercise of unlimited jurisdiction

Costs